I TOOK THE EASY WAY OUT

by

Thomas J. Day

Edited by Patricia Tallakson

I TOOK THE EASY WAY OUT

First Printing - March 2002

Author - Thomas J. Day
Publisher - McCleery & Sons Publishing

International Standard Book Number: 1-931916-02-0
Printed in the United States of America

Acknowledgements

I want to thank my family for their help in the content of this book and for the moral support they gave me in writing it. I especially want to thank Michael Day for persuading me to put some of my more unpleasant past into the book, Patrick Day for helping me with content (I believe that Pat threw out enough chapters to write another book), and Elizabeth Rajs for helping with content and being an assistant editor.

I also want to thank Benita Greff, Angi Simonson, and Mary Hannah Tanata for typing, editing, and encouraging me to write when I didn't want to.

Thanks to Reverend Paul Brunsberg for encouraging me for ten years to write this book.

I owe a special gratitude to all the people who took their time to write their personal stories for this book. I especially would like to thank Jim Marshall for contributing to this book and teaching me the philosophy of The Missing Link.

I also want to thank the chief editor, Patricia Tallakson, without whose help this book may not have been finished until Christmas 2002.

A special thanks to Tom Lehman, Jim Marshall, Boyd Christenson, and Jim Simle for supporting this book and to all the investors for giving me the time through funding to write this book.

Foreword

I am not a psychiatrist, psychologist, or a counselor, so this is not a professional book in an academic sense. All of the information in this book comes from my life experiences and the life experiences of others whom I have encountered on my journey to age sixty-five. Since July 21, 1977, I have been in a wheelchair because of a car accident, which broke my C4/5 vertebrae and crushed my spinal cord. I am paralyzed from the neck down, so I am a professional when it comes to living with a severe physical disability. No disrespect intended, but you cannot know what it's like to be in a wheelchair if you're able bodied and learning about it from a book.

Fortunately, or unfortunately as the case may be, my life has been less than uneventful. I have many experiences to share, and I have met thousands of people along the way with experiences to share. I'm the type of person that people tell their life stories to. Maybe that's because I am a person willing to share my most intimate experiences with all my friends. I am lucky because I have a lot of friends. I've heard people say that you're lucky if you have one or two good friends that you can count on. I have twenty or thirty really good friends who fit that description.

My career was selling life insurance, and I am a life member of the Million Dollar Round Table. That put me in the top five percent of all agents selling insurance. I learned a lot about psychology as a sales person. I was also a general agent for a large New York insurance company. And I learned a lot about hidden handicaps and counseling when I was training twenty to twenty-five agents. Also, I've had several severe hidden handicaps, including gambling, anger, and procrastination, which caused me to be a dysfunctional parent and husband. However, learning how to identify my hidden handicaps and overcome them has given me insight into how others can do the same.

I'm sharing my experiences with you in the hopes that those of you who are younger can learn from my mistakes and that those of you who are older will see that it's never too late to get rid of your hidden handicaps and live a happy life. Throughout the book, I suggest some ways to solve your hidden handicaps or at least identify them. In almost every case, I suggest that you go to a counselor, psychologist, or psychiatrist. Either way, reading this book is the first giant step in the right direction toward a happier life.

TABLE OF CONTENTS

Chapter 1
THREE MILES TO GLYNDON 1

Chapter 2
TAKE THE EASY WAY OUT 13

Chapter 3
TEN IS MORE THAN FOUR 29

Chapter 4
HIDDEN HANDICAPS 41

Chapter 5
HIDDEN HANDICAPS FROM 55
THE HORSE'S MOUTH

Chapter 6
BEAT THE MASTER AND TAKE THE FRESH 79

Chapter 7
OVERCOMING HIDDEN HANDICAPS 93

Chapter 8
WHEELCHAIR SHOCK 115

Chapter 9
BEHIND THE SCENES 129

Chapter 10
ATTENDANTS, SECRETARIES, NURSES, ... 137
COOKS, AND CHAUFFEURS

Chapter 11
EVERYONE SHOULD WRITE A BOOK 161

Chapter 12
DON'T GIVE UP, DON'T EVER GIVE UP 171

Chapter 13
WHO PUT THE TREE IN THE 187
MIDDLE OF THE ROAD

Chapter 1

THREE MILES TO GLYNDON

I awoke in a ditch, frantically tried to hit the brakes of my car, and slammed head on into a farm road going across the ditch. On impact, I was ejected from my driver-side door and hurled several feet from my car as it rolled away from me. The next thing I remember is lying in the ditch unable to move. After lying there for what seemed like an eternity, a truck driver stopped, and I begged him to help me up. He was smart enough not to move me and must have called an ambulance. I vaguely remember being put in the ambulance. Fortunately, I don't remember the next couple of days. During that time, I had surgery to repair my broken neck. Doctors took a piece of my hip and fused it to my fourth and fifth vertebrae. My injury is considered a very high spinal cord break.

I remember realizing that I was in a hospital room at St. Luke's in Fargo. What I didn't realize was that I had just begun my life as a quadriplegic. I also didn't realize what a long road I had ahead of me to accept and cope with this physical disability. My high spinal cord injury left me with only the use of the deltoid muscles in my shoulders. I can raise my arms to a certain degree, but I need gravity to lower them. But even more importantly, I didn't realize the hidden handicaps that I had been living with for most of my adult life, which were about to become more and more obvious to those who were close to me, people who worked with me, and eventually myself. A hidden handicap, which I will explain in-depth later, is something everyone has to some extent. A hidden handicap is any problem that is not visible to most people, which makes getting through the day difficult, such as depression, relationship troubles, alcoholism, etc. Later on in this chapter and throughout the book, I will talk about some severe hidden handicaps that I had been living with before the accident. The scary part about these hidden handicaps is that it took the accident and the road to recovery to realize that I had them and how significantly they were damaging my life. Overcoming these hidden handicaps turned out to be as hard as, or harder than, coming to grips with my physical disability. At age 41, I was not only paralyzed from the neck down, but, unknown to me, I was also paralyzed from the neck up.

During the first few days in intensive care, after I awoke, many of my friends wanted to come visit me, but the hospital only allowed relatives. You can't believe the number of uncles, cousins, brothers, and sisters that I acquired during that time. I have many nutty friends, and a lot of them talked their way in by passing as a relative. The most ingenious, however, was a friend I'll call Harold. Harold dressed up as a priest to get in to see me.

During my first three to four weeks in intensive care, I experienced hallucinations. I was going in and out of reality, and I can still remember the hallucinations very clearly. I believe being cut off from Doridan sleeping pills caused the hallucinations. When I was twenty-eight, I had an inner-ear infection. Every time I would lie down, the room would spin, so the doctors put me on Doridan, and I just never stopped using them. I had been addicted to Doridan for about thirteen years. I usually took two every night to get to sleep. (This is an example of a hidden handicap that I had before the accident.) After the accident, I was cut off from Doridan cold turkey. I was also a pack-a-day smoker, and being cut off from cigarettes might have also contributed to my hallucinations.

My recurring hallucination was that I had been hurt like this once before and was taken to Grand Forks, North Dakota, where they had healed me so that I could walk again. I believed this hallucination as if it were reality and was desperately trying to convey to my wife (Lynda), two brothers (Bill and Pat), sister (Kay), and son (Mike) that they needed to take me to Grand Forks. Because I was in intensive care, I was only allowed two visitors at a time. I couldn't talk about my delusions because my trachea and respirator did not allow me to talk. My family bought a game with letters in it to help me communicate. We worked out a system: if it was the correct letter, I blinked my right eye, and if it was the wrong letter, I blinked my left eye. Many times I got as far as "Take me to Grand Forks," and then I would try to say that in Grand Forks they could fix me so that I could walk. Every time we got that far, the two members of my family who were in the room at the time would decide that the message couldn't be "Take me to Grand Forks," so they would scramble all the letters and start over. I would go crazy inside. I would blink my eyes and make faces. They knew I was frustrated, but they didn't know why. My son, Mike, said that after they would scramble the letters, my eyes would eventually open wide and look like they were shooting laser beams at the two of them. Time after time, we would get "Take Me to Grand Forks," but we would never get any farther and they never got a whole message. It was a very frustrating time, but as we look back on it, we find it quite humorous.

At the time, I was on a Stryker frame bed, which was used to keep me from getting pneumonia. A Stryker frame bed is more excruciating than Chinese Water Torture. Every two hours, the nurses would strap me onto the bed with straps across my face, chin, chest, and legs and turn the bed upside down. I would then be hanging straight down. I couldn't feel anything from my chest down, but the straps on my face and chin would hurt tremendously. My family usually made it a point to visit when I was hanging down because they knew that it hurt and that talking to me distracted me from the pain. I also wore what is called a halo, which consisted of four large bars screwed into my skull and attached to the bed so that I couldn't move my head and neck.

In about ten days, I got off the Stryker frame, and it appeared I was recovering quite fast. They put me in a body cast so that they could hook up the halo to immobilize my neck and head. I was able to start getting in a wheelchair for a few hours a day, and the surgery on my neck was starting to heal. When I was in the wheelchair, they had me doing exercises through a machine to improve my breathing. The muscles in my chest were paralyzed, so I was breathing at half capacity. On one particular day, I was in my wheelchair using the breathing machine, and I told the nurse that I was really having trouble breathing. The nurse told me that I wasn't trying hard enough and to just keep going. Shortly after the nurse left the room, I went into cardiac arrest. Somebody at the nurses' station called in a code blue alert—the hospital's way of saying, "A patient is dying." They told me later that I would not have lived until the code blue team got there, but fortunately Dr. Holiday, the orthopedic doctor who had put my cast on, and Dr. Goltz, an eye, ear, nose, and throat specialist and close family friend, were charting at the nurses' station outside my door. The two doctors immediately came into my room. Dr. Goltz performed a tracheotomy, and Dr. Holiday had his tool with him to tear off my body cast. I was having trouble breathing because I had developed an advanced case of pneumonia.

The next thing I remember is waking up in Shanghai getting the Chinese Water Torture again. And, to add to the horror, I had about seven tubes coming out of my body—an intravenous tube, four chest tubes to drain phlegm out of my chest, a catheter, and a tube they left in my arm so that the nurses could come every morning to take blood samples. I was also back on the respirator and trachea. When they prepared to turn me over on the Stryker frame, all of the tubes had to be lined up so that they would turn the same direction I was turning. On several occasions, I could see that the tubes were going to go one way and that I was going to go the other. Unlike the first time I was on the respirator and trachea, this time I learned how to communicate while I was on them. I would make noises trying to alert the nurses and aides to let them know that we had a problem. Most of the time, they would correct the tubes, and the turn would go all right. However, several times I was turned, and some of the tubes were pulled out of my body.

I was on the Stryker frame for six to eight weeks. Every day I would ask my doctor when I could get off the Stryker frame, and he would tell me that it shouldn't be much longer. One day, to shut me up, he said I couldn't get off the Stryker frame until I got off the respirator. This wasn't entirely true, but I can understand how he got tired of me asking everyday. I immediately asked that he take off the respirator. The doctor said that I was not ready yet, but again I demanded that it be taken off. He finally gave in and told the nurses to take off the respirator, but he told them to leave it by my bed, as I would need it in a few minutes. I asked that they remove it from the room entirely. I found out later that he told the nurses to put it outside the door because I would need it again very soon. For the next three days, I thought every breath I took would be my last. But I didn't care because anything was better than the Stryker frame. After four or five days, when I was breathing on my own, I asked the doctor to get me off the Stryker frame, and he said that I also had to get off the trachea. I asked him to remove the trachea, which he did. Since it was helping me breathe, I had another rough two or three days. Finally, I was breathing completely on my own. Now the doctor had to tell me that he had said I needed to get off the trachea and respirator before I could get off the Stryker frame just to shut me up. He didn't think I could ever do it, and he apologized to me. I was very upset, but it turned out to be a blessing in disguise. Sometime later, I read my chart, and it said that I would never get off the respirator because my spinal cord injury was so high. Had I tried to get off of it *after* I got off the Stryker frame, I don't think I would have made it. A week to ten days later, I was finally able to get off the Stryker frame.

For the next three months, I went to physical and occupational therapy twice a day. The nights were still tough because I wasn't sleeping much. I had some great friends who would take turns spending most of the night with me. Although a lot of good friends visited me quite often, I had some friends who were conspicuously missing. One of them was a very good friend named Orv. He was afraid to come and see me because he didn't know what to say. One day he saw a mutual friend of ours named Maury, who lived about three hours from Fargo. Orv asked him what he was doing in town, and Maury told Orv that he was there to see me, which he did about once a week. Maury and I were Theta Chi fraternity brothers and had gone through initiation hell week together to become active members. This had created a very strong bond between us. Orv then realized that if Maury could drive three hours to see me, he needed to see me also. I can still see Orv coming through the door to my room. He was all shook up, and he told me that he didn't know what to say. He was scared, and he was sorry that he didn't come earlier, but now he was here. Orv is normally cocky, sarcastic, and very funny, and now here he was at my door looking like a jellyfish. I think I swore at him, made a few jokes, and tried to help him relax. I told Orv that my body didn't work anymore but that my mind was still the same as always. I reassured him that he could say anything to me just like he had in the past. After Orv relaxed, we had a nice visit, and he became a regular visitor, not only in the hospital but also in my house after I returned home.

When I returned home, my life was drastically different. Yes, I became a quadriplegic in a car accident, but before my accident, I was paralyzed from the neck up. I was a man with many hidden handicaps, a man who wasn't fully aware of all of his many personal demons and who thought he was living a great life. Before the accident, I did not fully realize what a negative impact my lifestyle was having on my wife and children. The signs were there that I should go to counseling, but I didn't go until after the accident.

I guess I should tell you a little more about myself and explain how the accident occurred before I explain what it taught me. I was born in Minneapolis, Minnesota, on March 11, 1936. I went to grade school and high school in Detroit Lakes, Minnesota. On December 17, 1960, I married Lynda in Redlands, California. We had three boys and two girls, who ranged in age from seven to fifteen when I had my accident. In 1964, I graduated from North Dakota State University in Fargo. I was in the life insurance business from 1964 until the time of my accident, which was on July 21, 1977. In 1974, I started buying old resorts and turning them into condominiums. My partners and I fixed up the resorts, added tennis courts, sailboats, canoes, etc., and then sold the cabins separately. In 1975, Bob Fortier and I started a T-shirt company called "The African Queen." We had several retail stores, but the main part of our business was manufacturing transfers for T-shirts. We sold these transfers retail and also supplied twenty-five to thirty retail shops with wholesale custom transfers and T-shirts. Besides trying to juggle three businesses, I played golf at least six times a week, usually thirty-six holes a day. I gambled on the golf course, and I played a lot of high-stakes poker. I also played tennis year round. With all of these activities plus socializing, I wasn't spending nearly enough time at home with my wife and children. I was operating in the very fast lane. Little did I know that the Lord had plans to slow me down.

On July 20, 1977, at five thirty in the morning, I got up and went to the Fargo Country Club. I had a seven o'clock tee time to qualify for the North Dakota State Amateur Golf Tournament. I ate breakfast at the club and then went to hit some practice balls. I shot a seventy-four to qualify for the tournament, and then I went to my office at The African Queen and worked until about five.

The African Queen sold large orders of iron-on transfers because the transfers were only about twenty-five cents each. If the customers bought one thousand transfers, they could buy the T-shirts as they sold them. We would lend them a heat transfer machine, and they would iron on the transfers as they sold the shirts. Our customers would never get caught with too many T-shirts because The African Queen repurchased any unused T-shirts. A few days earlier, I had sold a large order to a drug store in Perham, Minnesota. We had already sent the T-shirts, transfers, and heat transfer machine to Perham. I promised the owner that I would come to his store some evening the next week to help him set up the display. July 20th was the night I decided to drive to Perham to help my customer. My 1976 Buick Park Avenue was in the shop for repairs, so I drove to Perham in a loaner car. In Perham, I looked for the owner for about an hour, but I could not find him. I hadn't called ahead because Perham is such a small town that typically it is easy to find someone. On the way back to Fargo, I stopped in Detroit Lakes and made a call to an insurance client. He and his wife were free to see me, so I went over to have an interview and sold them some additional insurance.

On the way out of town, I stopped at a bar and restaurant called the Erie Junior. I got there between eleven thirty and midnight and ran into some friends. I visited with them for about an hour, but I didn't have any alcoholic beverages. When the bar closed at one, we went to the restaurant side of the Erie Junior for breakfast. At approximately two o'clock, I headed for Fargo, which is about forty-five miles from Detroit Lakes. I had now been up for more than twenty hours and was getting very tired. It was a hot night and the air conditioning in my loaner car didn't work very well, so I started to nod off. I was just getting ready to stop the car and walk around it a few times when I saw a sign: "Moorhead 12 Miles, Glyndon 3 Miles." I was sure I could make it to Glyndon, and from Glyndon, it is only six miles to Dilworth, three more miles to Moorhead, and then Fargo is right across the river. I never made it to Glyndon.

After my first six months at St. Luke's Hospital, part of my earlier hallucination came true—I was transferred to the rehabilitation hospital in Grand Forks. But no, they didn't get me to walk again! The therapy there wasn't any more helpful than the therapy in Fargo, and I didn't get nearly as much company. I asked to be transferred back to St. Luke's and remained there for about another month before I was released to go home.

While in the hospital and when I first moved home, my addiction to Doridan, which was a hidden handicap before my accident, had come back as a major hidden handicap. As I will explain in greater depth later, a hidden handicap is when an individual has a problem that is not obvious to other people and only obvious to the individual in various stages. A hidden handicap usually results in severe consequences. The first three months I was hospitalized, I was in critical condition and was not allowed any prescription drugs such as painkillers and sleeping pills. However, after I got out of intensive care, I didn't sleep well, so the doctors and nurses gave me my old friend Doridan every night. For the tremendous pain in my neck and shoulders, they gave me muscle relaxants, shots of pain medication, and painkillers. And when all this made me nervous, they gave me tranquilizers. I was on my way to becoming a drug addict before I left the hospital. When I got home, it got worse. As bad luck would have it, a doctor friend of mine called and asked what medication I was on and sent me samples to help me out. He had no idea I was abusing these drugs, so he sent enough pills for an army of drug addicts. As many addicts know, my worst fear was running out of drugs. So I ordered as many prescriptions as possible from various pharmacies, and they all gave me way too many drugs. I kept myself in a semi-conscious state so that I wouldn't have to face reality. I was taking eleven to twelve Doridan a day, four or five shots of pain medication, pain pills, and tranquilizers. I was able to do this by having everyone in the house—five kids, my wife, and two nurses—give me one or two pills a day. None of them knew the total picture.

One morning, I asked my nine-year-old son to give me one sleeping pill and two Bufferin. The Bufferin looked almost identical to the Doridan, and Joe gave me three Doridan by mistake. I never should have had Joe do this. But, because of my addiction, I would have used anybody to do anything. Shortly after I took the three Doridan, my attendant got me up in my wheelchair, and the Easter Seal therapist arrived. I was so out of it that I couldn't hold my head up or talk. I just mumbled. The therapist called for my wife and told her that there was something wrong with me. Lynda had been concerned about the amount of drugs I was taking, and she only knew about twenty percent of them. She went into my bathroom and found my hidden drugs. She flushed them all down the toilet, and my habit was stopped cold turkey. In two days, I was climbing the walls, which was quite a feat for me. I was put back in the hospital for drug addiction treatment.

Just like when I was cut off from Doridan at the time of my accident, I started hallucinating again. They tried to put me back on all of the drugs I was taking and then slowly decreased the dosage. You've heard of taking things one day at a time; when I got down to a quarter of a Doridan sleeping pill every two hours, I had to take things fifteen minutes at a time. When the nurses gave me my fourth of a Doridan, I felt all right for about half an hour. Then I started craving the next dose. I knew I couldn't make it another hour and a half, but I could make it another fifteen minutes, and another fifteen minutes. Soon enough I would get the next dose, and it would start all over again. I don't know how people on hard drugs such as heroin can get off them, but breaking the prescription drug habit might be just as bad. I know this much: I never want to go through that again.

Because of the two or three days I was cold turkey, the detox formula didn't work quite right, and I hallucinated for a couple of weeks. This time the hallucination was wilder than those I had experienced when I first went into the hospital. I thought all the nurses, doctors, and aides were using psychological warfare to get me. My room walls were painted with a stripe about a foot and a half wide about six inches from the ceiling. I thought the strip was a one-way mirror through which the doctors and nurses were watching my every move, trying to find ways to push me over the edge. Things that they did reinforced my hallucinations. For example, when they would dial telephone numbers for me and hold the phone to my ear, I would call friends and my kids with wild stories of what they were doing to me and beg them to come get me. So the nurses cut off my phone privileges. This reinforced, in my mind, that I was being held captive. I also would hear telephones ringing and thought my hand was a phone. I'd hear the phone ring and hold my hand to my ear and start talking. Lynden, who was my physical therapist and who has now been my friend for more than twenty-four years, didn't know how confused I really was, so he let me use his phone. On one of those calls, I convinced an attorney friend to come up and see me because they were torturing me. Fortunately, he called my wife and told her the story. She told him not to visit me, as I was out of my mind.

Diane in occupational therapy helped pull me out of my hallucinations. I went to physical and occupational therapy during the day. When she would see me talking to my hand, she would tell me that my hand was not a telephone and that I was not able to use a telephone. I could move my hand to my ear, but my lower arms and fingers were paralyzed. She would take a telephone, put it in my hand, and tell me to make a phone call. The phone would fall to the ground, along with my spirits, and then she would remind me again that I could not use a telephone. This helped to bring me back to reality.

During all of this confusion, I was going into the psych ward every day for treatment with other drug addicts and alcoholics. I was in a separate wing from the other addicts who stayed there twenty-four hours a day. I had to come and go, as they could not take care of someone with such a severe disability. I would get extremely nervous at night. The other addicts could walk around to get rid of nervous energy, but I could only lie in my bed. I had some real nice night nurses, though, and they would get me up in my wheelchair and take me to the occupational therapy room. One of the devices they had for quadriplegics was a set of pulleys. They strapped one on each of my arms so that I could go up and down with my arms. I did that for about an hour until I was so tired I couldn't move my arms anymore. Then the nurses took me back to bed, where my nervousness had decreased enough for me to go to sleep. I started doing this almost every night, and it really seemed to help. I completed the six-week treatment and was again released to go home to further deal with my physical disability and newfound hidden handicap.

I would find out on my return home that initially dealing with my physical disability would be extremely difficult. Through both necessity and luck, I would eventually discover the easy way to live with my physical disability. But it would take me a lot longer to find a way to overcome my hidden handicaps. As hard it was to overcome my physical disability, I would be amazed to find out that it was as hard, or harder, to overcome many of my hidden handicaps.

Chapter 2

TAKE THE EASY WAY OUT

Most people don't understand the difference between living life the easy way and living it the hard way. Distinguishing between the two can be very difficult. I am convinced that what most people think is taking the easy way out is actually the hard way to live and that what people think is the hard way to live is actually taking the easy way out. As an example of the hard way versus the easy way, let's look at my situation after I got out of the hospital following my accident.

When I first came home from the hospital, it looked like I was taking the easy way out, but it was really the hard way. I spent my days watching television, crying, doing physical therapy several times a day, and crying some more. A lady from Easter Seal would come each day to do occupational therapy, and then I would cry some more. I didn't have a van my first year home, so I wasn't able to go to any sporting events or watch my children participate in any of their activities. Some friends would come over to visit, but my self-esteem was so low that communicating with them was an effort. As much as I appreciated their visits, I actually dreaded them. Each day seemed about sixty hours long. I didn't sleep much, and the nights dragged on. No good programs were on television, and no programs were on at all after one in the morning because Fargo didn't have cable yet. At night, all I had to look forward to was another sixty-hour day. Nurses took care of me from eight to five every day. After that, my wife and five children took care of me. Getting used to someone feeding me, giving me a drink of water, brushing my teeth, and literally taking care of all of my physical needs was very hard. Even though I was a quadriplegic, some people might think I had it as comfortable as possible since I didn't have any responsibilities and all my needs were being met. But I thought life was extremely difficult and didn't know how I was going to continue. And nobody was praising me by saying, "Tom, you're doing a great job! I can't imagine how you get through each day."

In a strange twist of fate, my poor financial situation and poor insurance made it possible for me to start taking the easy way out. When I got hurt in 1977, I had very bad group insurance benefits with the life insurance company I was working for. The company I had just left had a million-dollar major medical policy and lifetime benefits for disability. When I switched companies, I assumed I would have good benefits since I was working for an insurance company. But I couldn't have been more wrong. Its major medical health plan had a $100,000 limit, which I went through in less than a year. In addition, its disability policy only had a two-year benefit. This company's group benefits were all changed within two months of my accident. I was happy to help everybody in the future, but the change didn't help me. However, I received excellent benefits from the car insurance policies for awhile, as my attorney and friend, Jim Cahill, was able to establish a new precedent with auto insurance companies. I was driving a loaner car, and Russ Buick was paying premiums on that policy. I also had a car insurance policy of my own, for which I was paying the premiums. Jim argued that both insurance companies should pay benefits since there were two policies and two sets of premiums were being paid. Both companies did pay, and I had plenty of money for several years. There were health insurance benefits and disability income coming from the auto insurance companies. There was money from the two-year group disability policy with my employer, and $1,000 a month from an individual disability policy. But after I had been in the hospital for almost a year and at home for six months, I realized that most of the benefits were going to run out soon and that I would have to be placed in a nursing home.

After finding out I was paralyzed from the neck down, I assumed that I could never work again, and all the counseling I had in the hospital reaffirmed that belief. I would hope that anyone reading this book who has a physical disability will get the idea that a lot more can be accomplished than what other people think and say can be accomplished. If I had continued to believe that I couldn't work, then I might never have been able to take the easy way out.

In order to take the easy way out, you have to think for yourself instead of letting your life be run by what other people tell you can or can't accomplish. In other words, you must avoid SNIOP. SNIOP stands for "Subject to the Negative Influence of Other People." For example, you fall victim to SNIOP when you let people blame you for something that goes wrong, when you believe people's negative opinions about you, or when you abandon a good idea regarding a new business or sales idea because your friends shoot it down. Have you ever wondered why some people, who don't seem to be smarter than you, make more money? Part of the reason is that they trust their own intuition and are not influenced by other people. You can learn from other people, but once you have accumulated all the information, you need to make your own decisions. The same principle applies to how we handle problems. In many cases, society influences how we handle problems. We are told that certain problems are traumatic. The truth is they don't always have to be. You can learn to handle large problems in such a way that they do not cause a lot of stress. One of the ways of doing this is to deal with the problem as it exists and not what you imagine it could be. Instead of worrying about the problem, do something about it. Worrying increases the size of the problem, and doing decreases the size. The way we handle most problems is by how we have been influenced by other people. The first rule to taking the easy way out is that you must condition yourself, or other people will condition you. Do not let other people negatively influence you.

Living sixty-hour days was an example of not doing something about my problem and living life the hard way. I sat in bed or my wheelchair feeling sorry for myself but doing nothing to solve my problems. Instead of worrying and crying about my problems, I should have been developing some solutions. In a strange way, I was lucky that I was running out of money. Running out of money led to my solution. If I had had money, I might still be putting in those sixty-hour days. Since the money was quickly dwindling and I didn't want to go to a nursing home, I had no other choice but to work again, or win the lottery. I didn't think my odds of winning the lottery were good, so I went back to work.

The catalyst to getting back into the insurance business was a phone call from Bill Swanston, Jr. His nickname is "Swanny." Diplomacy is not one of Swanny's longsuits. He called on the phone and said, "Day, I need a million dollars worth of term insurance." I said, "Swanny, I'm not really in the insurance business anymore, but I'll get Lynda to get you a quote, and we'll mail it to you." "I bought that wheelchair lift for your van so that you'd use it. Get out of your @#$*&$! bed, and get your @## over here yourself. Stop laying around feeling sorry for yourself, and get over here," was the reply. So, with Lynda's help, we put together a quote. And, with the help of my attendant, I got my @#$*&$! @## over to Swanston equipment. Swanny bought the policy, and I realized I could sell insurance again.

Once I started working again, I started taking the easy way out. Between taking care of a family of five and being responsible for my care, Lynda had not had time to sell new insurance policies, but she was servicing our current policyholders. In early 1979, we returned full time to the life insurance business. Things went much better than I could have imagined. In 1979, we made about $30,000, and in 1980, that doubled to approximately $60,000. In 1981, our income doubled again to approximately $120,000. I was so busy that I couldn't do everything I needed to do each day. Every day was now like six hours instead of sixty. My self-esteem was good. We didn't have financial problems, and I no longer had time to feel sorry for myself. I had gotten over the denial stage of my injury and had made peace with being in a wheelchair. Most importantly, I no longer thought in terms of what I couldn't do; I thought in terms of what I could do. Finally, I took the easy way out!

How can I be taking the easy way out when I am paralyzed from the neck down, have continual bladder infections, constantly fight pressure sores on my butt, and get colds that are hard to handle because I don't have use of the muscles I need to cough? I am taking the easy way out because I am working very hard and enjoying it. I started using my wheelchair accessible van and going to sporting events, parties, visiting friends, going out to eat, etc. I've missed very few of my children's extracurricular events. In other words, I am living a fuller life than many able-bodied people.

People tell me now how great it is that I am working, compliment me on how active I am, and say I am an inspiration to them. Many people tell me that when they are having a rough day, they call me, and it makes them feel better. That is all wonderful to hear. I hope that I continue to inspire people, but sometimes I don't think I deserve that much praise for what I am doing, and I wonder where was everybody when I was putting in sixty-hour days and crying myself through each day? I'm here to tell you that those were tough days and that the year in the hospital before that was even tougher. That's when I needed people to say, "Tom, we really admire what you're doing," and "We can't believe how you are getting through each day." That isn't what they said. They felt sorry for me and gave me encouragement, but they didn't praise me and tell me what an inspiration I was to them. Now, when I'm taking the easy way out by working and being active socially, now after having had the fun of watching my kids grow up and participate in extracurricular activities and watching my nine grandchildren grow up, now I am admired and called an inspiration. Don't get me wrong. It's not that I don't appreciate all the nice things that have been said; it's just that it is happening at a time when I don't need it as much as I did before I started working because now I'm taking the easy way out.

I can understand why people are inspired by how active I am and how I'm supporting myself. I am very grateful for the way they feel. In fact, I remember two people with disabilities whom I associated with before my accident and how much they inspired me. My point is that we need to recognize people who are living the toughest life possible, the people with hidden handicaps—the homeless, the unemployed, those on welfare, and others like me when I was in the hospital or during my first year at home. Getting through each day in these circumstances is a tremendous struggle. These are the people who truly deserve praise for making it through one more day. I'm not saying they deserve praise for what they are accomplishing, but they deserve praise for their struggle. These are the people who are really struggling, not those of us who are taking the easy way out.

Life throws most of us bad breaks at some time in our lives. Sometimes it is an illness or situation from which you can recover. Sometimes it is an illness or situation from which you cannot recover, such as the death of a loved one. In my case, it was an accident. And unless medical science comes up with some miracles (which now appears possible), I will continue to be a quadriplegic. The big difference between all of our tragedies is how we handle them. In a situation like mine, I didn't have a choice to be a quadriplegic or not. I went through some unbelievably tough times during the ten months I was in the hospital. But I was not a hero because I had no choice. Heroes are people who make a choice to do something they don't have to do. For example, people who risk their lives to save another's life are true heroes. They should be an inspiration to all of us. The only difference between me and someone else who went through the same experience as I is the way in which we went through it. I think I have done better than most people, but there are some people who have handled the situation better than I have.

One of those people who handled his disability better than I did was my friend Charlie Travnicheck. Charlie had muscular dystrophy. I helped Charlie for about thirteen years before my accident. He was in a class by himself. Charlie was forced into taking life the hard way, but he made it into the easy way with his attitude. Charlie, who lived in either a hospital or nursing home for approximately forty years, transformed that hard life into as good a situation as possible. Charlie could only move his head and his right thumb, but he was more active and touched more lives than any person with a disability or most able-bodied people I've known. He was truly an inspiration to me before I got hurt and still inspires me in the way I try to live my life now.

I want to tell you how brilliant Charlie was and how he coped with his disability. We were able to find an electronic device called The Genie that could be adapted to almost any disability. Charlie's Genie had a laser beam that went from point A to point B. Charlie could move his thumb in and out of that beam to run his TV, his lights, radio, and other things in his room. This gave Charlie some independence, but there were still a lot of things he couldn't do. However, Charlie focused on what he was able to do.

Charlie had a cigarette and candy stand, which was in the hall outside of his room at St. John's Hospital. There was also a money tray on the stand where people could pay for what they bought and make change. It was unbelievable to me that people would steal money and products from Charlie, but they did. (I would later find out for myself that people would steal from anyone, as I have had more than $50,000 stolen from me by a few bad attendants and some business partners.) So we had to bring the candy and cigarette stand as well as the moneybox into his room. Bringing the money tray and products into Charlie's room was a blessing. Charlie already had many visitors during the day, but now everyone who bought cigarettes or candy came in to visit with him.

Charlie went to movies, parties, horse races, etc. You name it, and Charlie did it. In the 1950's and 1960's, there was a nursing school connected to St. John's Hospital. All the girls who were studying to be nurses would take Charlie places in his wheelchair van. Sometimes ten or twelve of them would pile into his van to go to an outdoor movie theater. There was no shortage of people willing to take Charlie wherever he wanted to go in his van. I was one of those people who took Charlie to a lot of places. (All the information I gained about genies, wheelchairs, and wheelchair vans would come in handy after I was hurt.) Every year Charlie even threw his own birthday party. He would get a band and rent a bar and dancehall called the Merry-Go-Round. There would be huge crowds at these birthday parties, including doctors, nurses, student nurses, and a lot of other people who loved Charlie.

With all odds stacked against him, Charlie lived as rewarding a life as possible. He was happier using his limited resources in the hospital than many successful able-bodied people are in their lives. By working and playing as hard as he could, Charlie took the easy way out and found happiness. Charlie died before I was out of intensive care. I was never able to talk to him again after I became paralyzed, but I learned a lot from him about taking the easy way out.

Although Charlie and I appear to be heroes because we took the easy way out, our only choice was how to handle our severe physical disabilities. I am not choosing to live an extremely difficult life. I am just a person living an extremely difficult life the best way I can. A true hero is someone like Father Jack Davis, a missionary in Chimbote, Peru. Father Jack is someone I consider a real hero. I accept the fact that I am an inspiration to a lot of people and am very grateful that they think that way. I am appreciative for the win-win situation where they have gotten something from me and in return they have helped me emotionally, physically, and financially. But the reason I am not a hero is I don't have the choice of not being paralyzed from the neck down. If I had a choice to use my arms and legs and be able bodied again but chose to stay a quadriplegic, then I would truly be a hero. Not a very smart hero, but a hero nonetheless. I do have a choice on how to live my life in this disabling condition, and I have chosen a route of working to stay at home and be independent. Everyone has a different perception. In my mind, I have taken the easy way out, and in a lot of other people's minds, my struggle to remain independent appears to be the hard road and is inspiring.

On the other hand, Father Jack has a much larger choice in the type of life he could lead versus the type of life he is living. He has chosen to live his life in what appears to be the hard way. His life is one that only a handful of people have the heart and courage to live. But in Father Jack's eyes, he is living the easy life because he is following his calling to live the way he wants to. To illustrate, I am going to quote from the first chapter of a book written by Brother Gerald Muller, CSC, entitled "An Ordinary Man; An Extraordinary Mission." It is a story about Father Jack and the life he has chosen to live:

> He has spent twenty-six of his more than fifty years living and working with the poorest of the poor in a desert place where tourists are warned there is little to see and the stench is terrible. He is John E. Davis, a priest, pastor,

provider, protector and protestor for justice. He is an ordinary man on an extraordinary mission. How this North Dakota native got to Chimbote, Peru, and stayed there for more than a quarter of a century is an odyssey still unfolding. He has been robbed at gunpoint, stabbed by thieves, exiled because of terrorist death threats, slept in a different house every night for weeks and yet claims the poor people with whom he works have given him more than he has given them. With zeal and charm and friendly persuasion, he has brought hundreds of volunteers into his thankless apostolate and thousands of dollars' worth of food, clothing, medicine, and facilities to a people as poor as those in India but whose eyes are bright with faith and hope and whose hearts are warm with generous hospitality to others in spite of their needs.

Father Jack's missionary calling wasn't always clear to him. He initially signed up for five years in Peru. After one year, he almost returned to Fargo because he didn't think he could stand the conditions in Chimbote. Through endurance and duty, he finished his five years and signed up for another five. But, even at this time, he had not completely committed his life to Chimbote. He was forced to leave Chimbote when his name was number two on a terrorist hit list of priests and four priests were killed. After six months, he went back to Chimbote. But for awhile, he still had to sleep in a different hut every night. Finally, all the terrorists were captured, and he was again able to live in his own dwelling. During the six months he could not return to Chimbote, he realized that Chimbote was his home. He will stay there for the rest of his life.

The heroine of the missionary story is Sister Peggy, who has been in Chimbote for seventeen years helping Father Jack. Sister Peggy was born and raised in Ireland. She is a Presentation nun having graduated from the Presentation Sisters' Convent in Ireland. Sister Peggy, like Father Jack, made a choice to live and help the poor in Chimbote, Peru. If I were an able-bodied person, I would probably go to Chimbote for a few weeks to help Father Jack and see what the situation there is really like. From the several videos I've seen and the stories I've heard from Father Jack and other people who have been to Chimbote, there is no way I could be there for twenty-six years, or even one year. In my mind, Father Jack and Sister Peggy are the real heroes and heroines of the world, and there are others like them. They chose a hard road, but through the satisfaction that comes from serving others, they are living rewarding lives.

I consider my wife and children to be similar to Father Davis and Sister Peggy. Although my family did not take the easy way out, they are the true heroes. Because of my accident, they suffered many of the same losses I did. They could have chosen to live in a situation where they had more attractive alternatives. Lynda stayed seventeen years as my wife and caregiver when she had other choices. My children helped me as long as they lived at home and still return to help. Physically, I had no other choices, and I wanted to stay at home. But my whole family sacrificed to help me stay at home and give me the opportunity to take the easy way out. Their choice to make sacrifices makes them the real heroes, not me.

Taking the easy way out is a very difficult subject to explain, and it's something that I understand so well that I hope I'm doing a good job of explaining it to you. Had I not been forced for financial reasons to work, I might have stayed at home or gone to a nursing home. However, I'd like to think that if I had been able to afford to live at home without working, that I would have kept busy and accepted my disability like I have now. I'd like to think that I would have been as involved in all of my children's extracurricular activities as I have been while I've been working. And I'd like to think that I would have spent the extra time getting involved in non-profit organizations and leading the fight for disability awareness to help other people with disabilities and myself. I might have had the means to test my integrity in that way if I had won two lawsuits I was involved in. One lawsuit was a case against General Motors regarding a faulty door latch, which we felt contributed to my paralysis. I also had a case against North Dakota Workmen's Compensation that would have paid all my medical bills for life and given me several thousand dollars a month in disability payments. I lost both of the cases. In addition, before the accident, I had just transferred from one insurance company to another. Had I had the million-dollar major medical policy and the disability policy with lifetime benefits that were offered in my former company, I would be living a different life.

If one or two of the above scenarios had gone in my favor, I would have never had to work again. The way that I got over feeling depressed about the accident and losing those two lawsuits was by believing God had a plan for me. As I look back on the last twenty-four years, I certainly wish that the accident had not happened, but since it did, I think it has been a good life for me. I have met a lot of wonderful people because I've had to work. I've also gotten to know some wonderful college girls who've been my attendants. I've also discovered and eliminated many hidden handicaps in my life because of the accident. I don't think I would have discovered many of these if I had not had this disability. I believe I am in much better mental condition now than I would have been if I had not had this disability. Through the good financial times and the bad financial times, working has given me the best life that I could have under these circumstances. I certainly feel that by working I have taken the easy way out.

There's more to taking the easy way out than just working. You also need to have the right motivation for achieving your goals. The motivating force through most of the period that I have had this disability has been my desire to stay out of a nursing home. In the last few years, on the advice of my counselor and friend, Reverend Paul Brunsberg, I have tried to focus more on helping other people and finding goals to pay my own way rather than operating on the fear of going into a nursing home. Operating on fear alone is very draining. Four or five years ago, I was telling Reverend Brunsberg how hard it was for me to stay motivated to continue to earn the money needed to stay at home. At times, I wanted to stay home so badly that I asked people for more help than I should've asked for. I think they helped me because they saw how hard I was fighting to remain independent. I apologize if I've gone overboard, but at this time, I want to thank all of the people who have helped me to stay out of the nursing home. I am very happy to be living in my own home. Changing my motivation from fear of the nursing home to the desire to be at home helped me immensely. Anytime you can find a motivating factor that energizes you rather than drains you, you will be taking the easy way out.

Now that we've seen how what appears to be the hard way—working with the right motivation—is really the easy way, let's look at people who are actually taking the hard way out, which appears to many people to be the easy way out. Most people look down on alcoholics, homeless people, people on welfare, people on unemployment, people on disability whose disability doesn't seem that serious, and I could go on and on with this list. I hear people say that those people have a choice and that they are just lazy or that they do not want to work. Most people think they're taking the easy way out by living off the system. But who would want to trade places with them? I know that when we were children, some of us wanted to grow up to be baseball players, or firemen, or doctors, or nurses, etc. Did you ever hear a kid say, "I want to grow up to be homeless, an alcoholic, unemployed, or a bank robber"? There are a lot of circumstances that determine what we are when we grow up. I don't mean to say that we have no choices in our future, but a lot of things beyond our control affect what we become as adults. Among the most important factors are parents, peers, and home and school environments. Before we judge these people, we should ask ourselves, "Have I been molested by an uncle, a friend of the family, or my father or mother?" or "Have I had parents or a brother or sister give me drugs or alcohol when I was seven years old?" I could go on and on, but these are the things that have happened to many children and that affect what they become when they grow up. These are things that are hidden and could explain behavior that seems inexplicable. Having these things happen and living the lifestyles listed above is not taking the easy way out.

I have a physical disability that is very obvious to everyone, but there are many people who have handicaps that cannot be seen. They may have a situational depression or one that is caused from a chemical imbalance. They may have marital problems, financial problems, or claustrophobia, etc. As I said before, maybe the people who are failing or not doing as well as we think they should are the people we should pat on the back because we don't know what is going on inside of them to cause these shortcomings. We should try to find out what their problem is and then tell them that we realize what a struggle it is for them to make it through each day. Those of you who are doing well have no idea how hard their lives are. Before I got hurt, I was doing well and had no idea how these people were suffering. When we were playing golf and it was 72° with no wind, a fellow named Jiggs used to say, "I wonder what the poor people are doing?" I think of that a lot because now I *know* what they're doing. I know there are a lot of agencies out there trying to help these people, but they are only seeing the tip of the iceberg. In doing research for this book, I've talked to hundreds of people who have severe hidden handicaps and who are not receiving any help. I've gotten a lot of help because I have a physical disability that people can see. There are a lot of people out there who are hurting worse than I am and need help more than I do, but their handicaps are not obvious. We should look for people who don't seem to be doing well and attempt to find out why they are living the kind of life they are, which is in no way an easy task. But if we understand that those people are not taking the easy way out, then we can help them start to take the easy way out by offering encouragement and support instead of judgment.

On the other hand, it is up to people with non-physical disabilities or hidden handicaps to take responsibility and tell people about their problems. Some people have a hidden handicap that is so hidden they don't even realize they have it. These are the people who are really hard to help. Everyone should go to a counselor to help them identify their hidden handicaps. Free counseling is available for those who cannot afford to pay, and many other good counselors charge according to income. I'm not saying that this is easy, but those who want to overcome their hidden handicaps badly enough will find a way. I know how hard identifying hidden handicaps and going to a counselor can be because my kids and my wife were telling me about some hidden handicaps I had. I didn't know what they were, but I should have gone to a counselor just on the basis that people who loved me were telling me that I had some problems. I didn't go because I didn't think they were right and I didn't want them to be right. I didn't want to have to change because I was happy with my life as it was, or so I thought. However, since going to counseling, my relationships with my children, grandchildren, and friends have been much better, and my relationship with my ex-wife has also been better. Most of all, I feel better about myself.

I have one final comment about taking the easy way out. Attitude and common sense determine how tough or how easy your life will be. We constantly have problems each and everyday. These problems can be small, medium, or large. Whenever we have these problems, many thoughts run through our minds. Each thought is a possible solution to the problem. However, the thought that we take action on becomes our reality. We cannot change what other people will do or say, and we can't change certain events that will happen such as a blizzard or a tornado. What we can change is how we react to what people say or to events that happen. I believe that I control ninety percent of my life, but I have no control over the other ten percent. How we react to a situation decides whether it goes well, awfully well, so-so, bad, or awfully bad.

Let me give you an example. You come to work in the morning, and your partner makes a smart remark to you about a purchase you made yesterday. He tells you that you paid too much for the item. A lot of thoughts go through your mind, but you decide to take action on this thought, "You're right. I probably did." That's the end of it, and there's no problem. But let's say you decide to take action on another thought, and you say, "How about the three items you bought last week? You paid too much for all three of them." Then he yells back at you, and you yell back at him. Now you've got a real fight going. The end result could be anything from one day of not talking to each other and then having a talk and settling the matter, all the way to each person having said so much that you end up dissolving the partnership. Could you have stopped this fight right in the beginning? Yes, you could have simply agreed. Could your partner have stopped the problem much sooner? Yes, after you made your remark about how he spent too much on three items last week, he had plenty of thoughts going through his mind. If he would have said, "Yeah, I guess both of us should watch our spending," the fight could have been avoided. These types of things happen to us everyday. Make good use of the ninety percent of your life that you can control, have a good attitude, use common sense, and swallow your pride once in awhile. You will then have a happy and much easier life.

As you have read this chapter, you should have discovered that "take the easy way out" means that when you are handed a challenge, the way that you handle it determines how tough or how easy your life may be from then on. This book is meant to help as many people as possible, and in doing so, to help me find a new path in my life for happiness. At age sixty-five, I have constantly been working on becoming a better person. At first, I had so far to go that I was able to make some large strides. And even though I still have a long way to go, I learn a little bit more about myself every day, and I feel a little better each day. Even though I still make mistakes, they seem to be getting smaller.

So the moral of the story and the name of my book, "I Took the Easy Way Out," is that working hard and doing the right things is always the easy way out. In my case, even as bad as my physical disability appears, I'm taking the easy way out by working and eliminating my hidden handicaps. Sometimes the easy way out doesn't appear that way until you look at a person's alternatives. For me, it's either work or stare at the walls in a nursing home. At other times, when it may appear that someone is taking the easy way out, they may be silently and secretly going through misery. Only you really know if you are taking the easy way out, and it is up to you either to continue to live a life that is hard and unrewarding or to strive to do the best you can under your unique circumstances. If you choose to do your best, you will be taking the easy way out. This is a lesson that I learned the hard way in one of my college courses. It was an elective class for me, fortunately not a required course for you, as you will see in the next chapter.

Chapter 3

TEN IS MORE THAN FOUR

I started college at North Dakota Agricultural College (NDAC) in 1954 and graduated from North Dakota State University (NDSU) in 1964. I was there so long they had a name change. My behavior in these first three years of college led to the hidden handicap that eventually caused my accident. When I grew up in Detroit Lakes, I was mischievous, but I didn't cheat in school, and I never stole anything. I had never heard of drugs, and I didn't drink alcohol, so I was way ahead of my time as a designated driver. My unacceptable behavior in college was not the result of alcohol. It was a rebellion against a very ethical, strict father who was unable to express his love. The stories I'm going to tell you are stories from my past that I used to believe were interesting, and I was proud of never getting caught. Therein lies the problem: I never got caught. I now only have remorse for these stories and certainly do not recommend that anyone follow in my footsteps. It has only been within the past few years that I have realized this part of my life was the foundation for one of my worst hidden handicaps, the hidden handicap that led to my accident, paralysis, and many other problems in my life.

This hidden handicap began developing when I started stealing in college. During my freshman year, while I was playing football and basketball for NDAC, I engaged in several episodes that involved stealing. One of these happened after the NDAC Bison trainer went through all the athletes' lockers during Christmas vacation looking for liquor and stolen athletic equipment. We all felt this was an invasion of our privacy, and three of us retaliated by taking the hinges off two double doors that led to the equipment room. We took jerseys, T-shirts, sweatpants, sweatshirts, duffel bags, and a few other items.

What we didn't realize was that we had taken all of the T-shirts that said "Coach" on them. Our head basketball coach, Chuck Bentson, was very upset about this. The next time we went on a basketball trip, he had two of the three of us ride in his car, and the other players went in a small bus. It was about a three-hundred-mile trip. For most of the trip, he told us that he knew we were the ones who had broken into the equipment room and that taking his T-shirts was what really made him mad. He kept trying to get us to admit to doing it. We never did, and he couldn't prove it.

On another occasion, we went on a trip to Brookings, South Dakota, to play SDSU in basketball. This was in the early fifties, and our dressing room was an Anatomy classroom. In the front of the classroom, hung a human skeleton. My roommate and I thought that the head would look good hanging in our bedroom. My roommate was able to get the skull into his duffel bag, and the next day the skull was hanging in our bedroom at the Theta Chi House. The following Monday, Coach Bentson called me over to his office and said that SDSU had called and wanted the head to their skeleton back. He told me he was sure that I knew where the head was and that he wanted it in his office that day. He said he'd leave his door open and if the skeleton head was in there by the end of the day, there would be no punishment. Needless to say, I brought it back, and there was never another word about the incident.

On another basketball trip to Sioux Falls, South Dakota to play Augustana College, we again stole without any significant consequences. After the game, the two other fellows who were involved in the above escapades and I went to a bar in downtown Sioux Falls that had a good four-person musical group for entertainment. Every hour the group members changed outfits. The second hour they came out in white sport coats with big black musical notes on them. We decided we had to have those sport coats. The next time they went to change, we followed them. Their dressing room was right next to the men's room. After they came out in their new outfits, we went back to their dressing room, which was open, and took three coats into the men's room. We locked the door, put on the sport coats, and put our big winter coats over them. We then walked out the door as owners of three new sport coats. Several weeks later, the three of us decided to wear these coats to a Theta Chi formal party. We were triple dating and having supper at a fancy restaurant to start out the evening. Two of us were going steady with our dates, but the other guy was taking out his girl for the second time. We didn't tell the girls what we were wearing, and our winter coats covered the sport coats. When we got to the restaurant, our two dates laughed, although they were a little embarrassed. The girl going out with our buddy for the second time took one look at him, put on her coat, and left. All I can say about the rest of his evening was that his date was a drink in his right hand. Even though our buddy suffered from this escapade, I still did not suffer any consequences and only saw his situation as comical.

My behaviors in college that led to my hidden handicaps involved not only stealing but also cheating. The first time I cheated in a class was in Algebra. I talked to the teacher after the midterm, and she said I needed an A or a B to pass the class. If I didn't pass the class, I wasn't going to be eligible for football. There was no way that I could have passed that test with the short amount of time that I had to study for it. I was good at accounting-type math, but very poor in Algebra, Calculus, etc. A friend from Detroit Lakes nicknamed "The Snipe" was a whiz in math, so I asked him if he would help me get an A on my Algebra final. I told him what I wanted him to do, and he said he'd do it. He went to my instructor and told her he had just returned from the service and was going to major in engineering. He said it had been three or four years since he had taken Algebra, and he wondered if he needed to take it again or if he still remembered it well enough. He asked her if he could take the Algebra final, and she said, "yes." When she showed him the schedule of her tests, he of course chose the time that I was taking my final. The teacher used alternate tests, and he sat in the back of the class where he would have the same test as I did. About half an hour before the two hours were up, I had another friend knock on the door and tell the teacher that he had an important message for someone in the class and wondered how long it would be before the test was over. During this diversion, The Snipe got up and walked by me, and we exchanged tests. I put my name on the test, turned it in, and left. I got an A on the final and a C in the class. There's a little more to this story. The Snipe had to redo my test so that he could turn it in to the teacher. The girl sitting next to him was the sister of a good friend of ours. We also knew her pretty well. She had seen what happened and told The Snipe to do her test, which was an alternate, or she would turn us in. So after he finished the test I had handed him, The Snipe quickly did her test. She also got an A on the final. Again, the consequences of cheating were non-existent for me, or so I thought.

My cheating wasn't limited to my own personal gain. In Freshman English, which was required for all students, the professors gave us five hundred words to learn to spell. Each quarter we had to take a test of one hundred words from that list. In the first quarter, we had to get eighty out of one hundred to pass; in the second quarter, we had to get eighty-five out of one hundred; and in the third quarter, we had to get ninety out of one hundred. We could not pass the course until we had passed the spelling tests. If we failed it the first time in our own classroom, we then took it again in a big classroom with all of the students from the other English sections who had also failed. If we failed again, we needed to take the test again and again until we passed. I was very good at spelling, so I got paid to go to the big class and take someone's test for them. Our English teacher did not distribute the second test, so the person giving the test did not know who we were. Sometimes I would bring two blue books and complete the test for two different people. One of the times I did this, I was taking the test for another football player. He had failed to mention to me that when he took the test the first time, he only got three or four right. When I took the test for him and got around eighty-eight words right, his instructor knew something was up. She called him into her office and gave him the same one-hundred-word test that I had just passed in his name. This time he got five or six right. At that point, she commented that she didn't know how he did it, but she was personally going to see that he got kicked out of school, and he did. For some unknown reason, he never let the teacher know I was involved. This was a pattern that continued to happen to me. I always got away with things. In the end, getting away with things turned out to be disastrous.

As I grew confident about my ability to escape the consequences of my actions, my actions became even more daring. A fellow jock nicknamed "The Hood" and I went into the business of stealing schoolbooks, slide rules, and tests. At first, we just took orders for schoolbooks and slide rules, stole them, and then sold them to the students for half price. It seemed like every student on campus knew about our activities. Then The Hood and I started stealing our own tests. Pretty soon we were getting orders to steal tests for other people. We had several methods of stealing tests. One was getting to know the secretaries in various departments and getting copies of the tests from them. When that failed, we would pick the lock at Minard, which was the main classroom building at NDAC at that time. After we were in the building, we would pick the locks on some doors, and when that didn't work, we would crawl through the transoms. If that failed, we would take the pins out of the hinges and remove the whole door. At first we were doing this for just a few friends and ourselves. Pretty soon it became a big business. People would come to us from all parts of the college with orders for tests. During test week, I would go two or three days and nights without sleep. In fact, I remember one quarter that ended just before Christmas. I had practically no sleep the whole week. Two days before Christmas, I went over in the morning to take the last of my final tests. After the test, I was so tired that I could hardly make it back to my dorm room. I flopped down on the bed with my winter coat on and didn't wake up until about two the next afternoon, more than twenty-four hours later. Everyone else was gone, and I had no idea what day it was. I found out it was Christmas Eve, and I barely made it back to Detroit Lakes for Christmas Eve supper. My parents were worried because they knew that school had ended the day before, but still no one knew what was going on, and I did not get caught.

I joined the Theta Chi Fraternity when I first came to college, and spring quarter I started living in the fraternity house. The test stealing continued for several years, and I made a lot of money doing it. People from other fraternities and other students on campus would come to us with orders and pay us large sums of money for the tests.

The Kappa Psi Fraternity (all pharmacy students) had a lot of the same tests, so ten or more pharmacy students would each chip in for one test, and we made even more money.

One particular quarter, a fellow in our fraternity needed an A on his math final to get a C or D in the class. He had a girlfriend at school, so he didn't want to leave. But his dad was supporting him and said that if he didn't improve his grades, he was cutting him off. He came to me and offered me a lot of money to steal his test for him. I wasn't able to get it, but the money was so good that I devised a risky plan to complete the task. I hired three students who had already taken the class (one was The Snipe again) and put them in a room together. Two were to work the math problems, and the third was to write them in the blue book so that they were all in the same handwriting. I stood outside the classroom where the final was going to be taking place. As soon as the teacher passed out the tests, I knocked on the door and told the teacher that I had an emergency message for Charlie that needed to be personally delivered. I was wearing a trench coat when I walked up to Charlie, and as we talked, he put the test against my chest. I closed my trench coat and walked out the door. Now Charlie was sitting there with scratch paper and a blue book, but no test. I ran it over to the dorm room where the three minds were waiting. They finished the test in no time at all, and I took the test and a blue book back to the classroom, knocked on the door, and told the teacher I had another emergency message for Charlie. She was not very happy, but she let me talk to him one more time. As I bent over to talk to him, I dropped off the test and blue book and left the room. Charlie got an A on the test and a C for his final grade and was able to remain in school.

Needless to say, Charlie got in trouble again with another math course and offered me another large sum of money to do the same thing. The scenario was exactly the same, except for one detail. It had been awhile since the three minds (the same three who had done the last test for Charlie) had taken this class, and it took them longer to complete the test. While they were working on the test, Charlie was in the classroom sweating blood. All of the other students had finished the test, and Charlie was sitting there pretending to do problems on his scratch paper and writing things in his blue book, but he didn't have a test. Finally, the instructor said that he had to start correcting the tests, so Charlie would have to bring his test up to his office and finish it up there. As Charlie was walking down the hall and starting up the stairs, I came in the door and up the stairs next to him, and we did a hand off with the test and blue book through the stair railings. Charlie again received an A on his final and a C in his course, but Charlie almost had a heart attack, and this method was never tried again.

However, I continued to steal tests for money. One quarter, the Kappa Psi fraternity decided that they didn't need to pay me to get their tests. They would steal them on their own. I knew the two students who were going to try to steal the tests, and they were not suited for the task. I went to the house to try to talk them out of it. It wasn't the money. I just figured that they would not be able to complete the job and, most importantly, would get caught. After a couple of years, I had become an expert at stealing tests. I had specific rules. I would never go into a room if I had to break anything or leave any trace that I had been there. I also never took a numbered test. I had a camera with a flash bulb and would take pictures of the test. I would make sure that everything was left in the exact order I had found it. Unfortunately, I could not talk these guys out of trying to steal the test and what happened to one of them was a shame. First of all, to get into the room, they broke a part of the door. So now the teacher knew someone had been in the room and began looking for clues to determine who it was. One of the guys dropped his glasses in the room in his haste to get out of there. It only took a few days to track the prescription to the individual. His punishment was very severe. They took away all of his college credits so that if he went to another school, he would have to start over. He also could never be a pharmacist. I don't know for sure what happened to him, but I don't think he ever went back to college. What happened to him was a ·shame, but by getting caught, he learned a lesson that may have made him a better person for the rest of his life. I am convinced that had I been caught, the rest of my life would have been completely different.

I was certainly doing some very bad things, but I was so clever that I was fooling myself and others into believing that I wasn't a bad person. For example, a female friend of mine had to give a speech about the most unforgettable character she had ever met. Her speech was about me, and, although names were not used, half of the class knew she was talking about me. She spoke about some of the crazy things I had done and then concluded her speech by saying that this person was a nice guy. The teacher ripped her speech apart and asked her how anyone who did those things could be a nice person. The other students came to the student's defense and told the teacher that the person she was referring to was a pretty good guy. The teacher never bought it and gave the girl a C for her speech. Two quarters later, I took the same class from the same teacher. I was good in speech, and I made sure I attended every class. I aced the tests, and the teacher and I got along great. When the class was over and I had received an A, I went to the teacher and told her that I was the subject of the unforgettable person speech my friend had given two quarters before. She was a good sport about the whole thing and told me that I was a pretty nice guy, but she did not condone any of the things I had done. Here was another one of my con jobs.

It appears that I was good at getting away with things. In order to stay eligible for football, basketball, and track, I passed my own courses through cheating. I made a lot of money helping other people cheat, and I never got caught. I got hurt in football in the middle of my sophomore year and was never able to play college football again, although I did play a year of varsity basketball. After my injury, I went to school off and on. In 1958, I quit school and went to California with a friend for what was going to be a couple of months but ended up being four years. I got married in California, and we had a boy named Mike. The three of us came back to Fargo in 1962, and that fall I enrolled at NDSU (the name had changed). I found out that after going to college for approximately four years I still had about two and a half years of school left. I took about twenty credits a quarter, went to every class, and studied. I also worked forty hours a week. This appeared to be the hard way, but it was actually the easy way. During those two years, I had a 3.5 grade point average, which brought up my overall GPA to a 3.0. All of my cheating just turned a four-year degree into a ten-year project.

Those of you who are cheating now, don't think that you're getting away with anything. You're hurting your fellow students who are studying, but you're mainly hurting yourself. If you're cheating in high school, you're not going to be ready for college. In college, you're paying for your education, so you're cheating yourself, and you won't be ready for your profession when you graduate. But the worst thing that can happen to you is, if you get away with it, it may come back to haunt you like it did me. You may continue to cheat in later life and get caught when the penalties will be much more severe. Trust me. Don't cheat. You'll feel much better about yourself if you don't.

I am sure that my cheating, stealing, and other wild behavior in my first several years of college was the reason it took me ten years to graduate. Many of these acts were very dangerous, and it is amazing that I never got caught. The fact that I didn't get caught became a hidden handicap buried in my subconscious mind. I thought I was invincible and could do anything without suffering any consequences. I never consciously thought I was Superman, but why else would I continue to do things that were dangerous and could have led to criminal prosecution, severe disability, or death? I haven't even mentioned some of the dangerous things I did while water skiing, swimming, driving, etc. This gambling with life continued on and eventually led to a literal gambling problem, my greatest hidden handicap, which will be discussed in more depth later in the book. With all the things that happened to me, including the accident, it wasn't until I lost my insurance licenses that I realized that I was not invincible. Prior to that, I had been operating on a subconscious level as if I were invincible. I must be kind of a slow learner. I'll guarantee you that I don't think I'm invincible any more, consciously or unconsciously. I realize how precious life is, and I'm doing everything in my power to make the best of the time I have left.

This subconscious feeling of being invincible caused me to do many irrational and dangerous things, and ultimately led to my accident. For years, I had driven when I was extremely tired, not drunk but tired. I fell asleep and almost went into the ditch at least thirty times and went into the ditch at least ten times. I never got hurt, so all I did was laugh about it and never changed the pattern. The worst instance prior to my accident that I remember was one night after driving home to Detroit Lakes while extremely tired. I did not remember driving the last thirty miles or going through the towns in that stretch. I woke up about four hours later parked in front of my parents' house with the hot sun beating in my car window. My last recollection was a town thirty miles outside of Detroit Lakes. Again nothing happened, so it was a joke to me. How is it possible to be any dumber than that? If some place along the line I would have learned a lesson, then the night of my accident I would have stopped the car and walked around awhile to wake up. This feeling of being invincible definitely caused my accident. I was driving again when I was extremely tired and didn't stop to rest. I had done this on so many other occasions but had always reached my destination in good health. This time I reached a different destination. It was St. Luke's Hospital, and I was paralyzed from the neck down for the rest of my life, which at this time has been more than twenty-four years. It was an extremely serious hidden handicap, which led to an extremely serious physical disability, which in turn led to more hidden handicaps.

I would like to help you and others avoid the same pitfalls that I fell into and realize the tremendous impact that things done when you're young can have on the rest of your life. Early behaviors can cause hidden handicaps that you don't realize exist until you get into your forties and fifties and look back on your life. If those of you reading this book could look back on your own lives with a fresh and open mind, you might realize that some destructive behavior in your past was caused by a hidden handicap, which in turn has led to new hidden handicaps that you still may not understand. What's the lesson in this for you? You really need to understand why you have fallen into a hidden handicap to be able to overcome it. Many of us come from dysfunctional families, which can cause hidden handicaps. After you realize what your problems are, you need to go back to your childhood family and find out what baggage you brought out of that family and dumped into your current life and family. When you realize why the hidden handicap developed, it's easier to correct your dysfunctional behavior. Unfortunately, this behavior affects everyone around you and causes your wife/husband and children to become dysfunctional. So if those you love are reacting negatively to you, instead of blaming it on them, look deep inside yourself to see what you are doing to cause their hostility. This is where you look for hidden handicaps. Go to counseling and get help before people walk out of your life. Please don't take as long as I did because it's not the easy way out for anybody. You can begin to do this by reading the rest of this book, talking with friends, and going through counseling.

Before moving on to the next chapter, I would like to apologize to all the past and present professors, staff, and students at NDSU for my extremely unethical behavior described in this chapter. I voluntarily included this information. It was not an easy decision, but these actions led me to where I am today. If I hadn't been honest and included this chapter, I would have had to lie to explain the rest of the book. But as I've learned and as I've been trying to stress, lying is taking the hard way out; therefore, by telling the truth, I'm following my path today and taking the easy way out.

Chapter 4

HIDDEN HANDICAPS

My handicap shows. Does yours? Most of you have a hidden handicap, and some of you have a combination of hidden handicaps. These handicaps keep you from reaching your full potential and cost you thousands of dollars each year. Most of these handicaps don't show, and the person with the handicap usually doesn't know about it, hasn't admitted that it's a problem, or is too embarrassed to tell other people about it.

As a quadriplegic who has worked for more than twenty-four years, I have come to believe that hidden handicaps can be harder to overcome than physical disabilities. Some people believe that my physical disability is more difficult to overcome than their hidden handicap because they cannot relate to what my handicap is like. However, hidden handicaps can be harder to deal with because most people have either told no one or just a few people about their problem. So they go through each day struggling with their hidden handicap and suffering through their work, family, and social life. No one is patting them on the back and telling them what a great job they are doing. So they are suffering alone, without a cheering section. I, on the other hand, with my physical disability am getting all kinds of praise and reassurance.

The second time I realized how devastating hidden handicaps could be was about seven or eight years ago when I met a man named Jerry Maxwell. I was going to do a motivational seminar for sales people in the insurance industry. A mutual friend introduced me to Jerry Maxwell as someone who would be a good candidate to do the seminar with me. Jerry lives in the Minneapolis area, and I went to visit him. After some initial conversation, Jerry shared his story with me. He had owned a medical supply business that was growing by leaps and bounds. It was actually growing too fast, and Jerry was short of capital, even though sales were rapidly increasing. Jerry said that he drove expensive cars, belonged to country clubs, and smoked expensive cigars, which added to the financial problems of the company. He had been promised a big loan by a Wall Street firm, but that fell through. His company fell apart, and he lost everything. Jerry said the worst thing about it was that all of his good friends had invested in the company, and he went into a deep depression because he felt so badly for what he had done to his friends and to himself. Fortunately, for Jerry, he had good disability insurance that paid $5,000 or $6,000 a month in disability income. He had told his story about how disability income had saved his financial life to many disability insurance agents and their clients and had even spoken at several national insurance conventions, so we began planning a seminar together. Near the end of our meeting, Jerry said something to me that will stick in my mind forever. He said, "Tom, don't take this wrong, but sometimes I wish I had a disability like yours. People can see what is wrong with you, but they can't with me. Some days I am so depressed I can hardly come out of my room. People look at me and wonder why I'm not working." It was true that he looked as healthy as a horse, and I never would have realized he had this problem if he hadn't told me about it. He told me that just talking to me that day was extremely painful for him and that when he gave a seminar, it took him about a month to build up the energy to do another one. Again, I realized how unbelievably difficult it can be to overcome hidden handicaps.

One of my hidden handicaps that made my life more difficult, which I didn't have until I went into the insurance business and didn't overcome until after my accident, was my fear of public speaking. In high school and college, I had taken every speech class possible, acted in plays, and done skits at pep fests. I had no fear at that time. After college, I went into the life insurance business and was very successful. Several years after I started with Mutual Benefit Life, I was asked to go to New Jersey to give a talk for a first-year agents leader convention. I flew to Newark a day before the convention.

When I got there, I started getting nervous about giving the speech. As the time for my speech grew closer, I became more and more nervous—almost to the point of panic. I gave the speech and was told it was a great speech. As a result, I was asked to give more speeches. I gave five or six more speeches at national meetings that were all hailed as great talks; however, I did not enjoy any of those meetings until my speech was over. I avoided giving seven or eight more speeches. Had I given all of these speeches, it would have enhanced my career with Mutual Benefit Life significantly. As a general agent and sales person for Mutual Benefit Life, I was giving up an opportunity that other sales people would have killed for. I still did well in my profession, as you will read later, but I didn't take advantage of a situation because of a hidden handicap, so I didn't do as well as I could have.

My fear of public speaking also kept me from being as involved as I could have been with Team Makers, a booster club for the North Dakota State University Bison. NDSU is my alma mater and where I played football, basketball, and track. I was and still am a big booster of athletics at NDSU. In approximately 1964, the Bison hired a new athletic director and new football coaches. It happened to be the start of national success for Bison athletics. The athletic director wanted me to head up the Team Makers' fund drive because Team Makers had never raised much money in the past. I told him to get somebody else to be the fund drive chairman and that I would help. I ended up doing ninety percent of the work, and we had a drive that raised five or six times the money that had ever been raised before. The people at the top knew who had done the work, so the following year I was asked again to be the fund drive chairman. I declined and ended up doing most of the work again anyway. Why was I refusing the job and the credit but doing all the work? Because the fund drive chairman automatically became the president of Team Makers the next year, and the president had to emcee the Team Makers' meeting every week during the school year. I could have done it. But I was afraid, so I didn't want to. Sadly, my fear of public speaking kept me from participating fully in an activity that I was committed to. I could give many other examples of how this hidden handicap has affected my life negatively. I don't have this fear anymore, maybe because I don't stand up in front of the audiences.

It didn't take me long to discover that I am not the only one whose life is being affected negatively by hidden handicaps. Before I began writing this book, I talked to many people and explained the concept of hidden handicaps to get their reactions. Many of them identified hidden handicaps in their own lives. One gentleman in particular, a friend for more than thirty-five years, shared with me a story about his own hidden handicap. Jack had never been one to share his feelings. I knew some of his problems, but only because they were so obvious to me. Back in the 1960's and 1970's, he made $200,000 to $300,000 a year running a large sales organization for a national company. Needless to say, this was huge money to earn at this time. He continually won every award that his company had to offer. Jack admitted how good he felt about himself in those days and how he enjoyed all of the accolades and praise that he received from everyone in the organization. He put some money away in various investments and is still comfortable financially. After 1985, his business became a victim of the computer age. In an effort to retain his investments and with continued drive, he spent the next fifteen years looking for another selling career. Jack has gone from selling job to selling job, getting himself all fired up for the product, and then losing his convictions because it was not the right opportunity. The last job Jack had, he was doing a great job of selling. However, he was working for some people who were short of capital, so he didn't receive his commissions in a timely manner, and finally he did not receive them at all. I think this experience broke his already fragile spirit. When I was telling Jack about hidden handicaps, he said, "Tom, it sounds like you are talking about me. I have low self-esteem, financial problems, and marital problems." Jack agreed that the praise and recognition he received during the good times were wonderful, but now was the time when he needed that encouragement the most. I told him that this was the time he should be getting awards and medals for making it through each day. I said I admired him for how hard he was fighting to make things work. Jack appreciated that I recognized his fight. Sometimes when you are so near the bottom, it is very hard to pull yourself up and regain control. Jack had never shared his innermost feelings with me, but our conversation led him to say, "Tom, I'm going to tell you something that I have never told anyone. As you know, I am a very devout Catholic and could never commit suicide, but in the last few years, when I go to bed at night, I pray that I won't wake up in the morning." At this moment, I realized that simply talking about hidden handicaps had helped Jack admit and talk about some of his own.

I also talked to Shawn, another friend, about my book and the concept of hidden handicaps, and he also thought I was talking about him. Shawn is a recovering alcoholic. He hasn't had a drink for about ten years, and his life is good. Shawn said now that people know he is a recovering alcoholic, they compliment him on overcoming the addiction and on how well he is doing. Shawn likes the praise now, but he admits that when he was drinking and everyday was hell, there was no one telling him how amazing it was that he made it through every day. Shawn said he didn't grow up as a child dreaming about being an alcoholic; it just happened. He hid the addiction from everyone for years. Between the struggles of trying to work, drink, and keep his secret, it was a much harder life than he has today.

After talking with these and other friends and thinking about my own life, I realized that everyone suffers from hidden handicaps of one sort or another such as low self-esteem, fear of public speaking, alcohol and drug addiction, negative family situations, financial problems, fear of failure, call reluctance, burnout, depression, fear of rejection, bad back, anger, headaches, insomnia, extra-marital affairs, claustrophobia and all the other phobias, stress, and procrastination. This is only a partial list of hidden handicaps, and the last two, stress and procrastination, are probably two of the most common because they are usually a part of all the others. Stress and procrastination are also two of the toughest ones to overcome. They are usually triggered by another handicap and are not always easy to identify.

I, and many people I know, suffer from the hidden handicap of procrastination; however, that wasn't always the case for me. For the first fourteen or fifteen years after my accident, I worked from nine in the morning to nine at night Monday through Thursday, nine to five on Friday, and half days on Saturday and Sunday. Procrastination was no part of my life. In the last seven or eight years, procrastination has become one of my biggest enemies. The main reason I procrastinate is that I don't like the jobs I'm doing. Procrastination is one of the most brutal of all hidden handicaps. I think it affects sales people to a higher percentage than most other jobs or professions because if you procrastinate selling, you don't earn an income.

In sales, procrastination is usually tied into call reluctance. See if this story sounds familiar to you. You are a commission salesman, and on Thursday you realize you've had a bad week. You decide it's too late in the week to do anything about it, so you plan to have a big week next week. Now this decision makes you feel better Thursday, Friday, Saturday, and Sunday. Monday morning you're going to get on the telephone and make a ton of appointments. Monday comes, and you have a couple of loose ends to tie up before you start calling. Then you make your calling list and look up all the telephone numbers. By now, it's too late to do much on Monday, so Tuesday morning you're going to start calling. Tuesday morning you actually start calling, and you don't find many people in their office. You finally get one appointment, and it's time for lunch. You come back from lunch at two o'clock and have some phone calls to return. You make a few more calls for appointments. No one says yes, but you have some callbacks for next week. Tuesday is now shot. Wednesday morning you start making calls, and you get another appointment. A friend calls to ask you to play golf. By now, you would have accepted an invitation to play Chinese checkers or go watch paint dry, so naturally you can't refuse an opportunity to go play golf. Lunch, getting ready to play golf, and the golf game itself eats up the rest of Wednesday. Now comes Thursday. You don't feel very good about yourself, so you find some paperwork that needs to be done. Then you make the decision that this week is shot and next week you are really going to get a bunch of appointments and have a big week. Now you feel reasonably good again, and you semi enjoy Friday, Saturday, and Sunday. Next week is similar to last week, and so it goes. The longer it goes, the harder it is to break out of this con job we're performing on ourselves. I believe it's easier to lie to ourselves than to anyone else. Sooner or later you break out of this trap, or you fail at sales. Some people never break out, and they do fail.

More and more people are working out of an office at home. I am one of those people, and I know that an office in the home has a lot of advantages—no time wasted in going to work and coming home, casual dress, all of your office machines available twenty four hours a day, seven days a week, and others. The pitfall is letting personal problems and duties interfere with work-related duties. It's a lot easier to procrastinate when working out of your home. As I mentioned previously, procrastination is usually the result of another hidden handicap such as call reluctance, stress, depression, avoiding any task that you don't want to complete, and many others.

My partner in the long distance business and best friend, Marv, called today. He told me he was having trouble getting himself to finish certain business tasks. He said he had been having more and more trouble forcing himself to get things done in the last month. Marv and I talk to each other about everything, or apparently almost everything. He had not talked to me about this problem before. After he wrote a long distance application, he was having trouble completing it and sending it in to Sprint. I told him that I had this problem a lot. I told Marv that what I do is write down three or four things I need to do today in order to make money and do them. He was doing the same thing that I have done on many occasions, finding all kinds of paperwork and avoiding doing the work needed to make money. Does this sound familiar to any of you? If this happens to you, do what I told Marv to do, and what I do myself. Don't do anything except the tasks that you write down as most important for today. If you are willing to sit there and do nothing, then you had better go to counseling. Usually, you'll do the things you need to get done, which won't be as hard once you get started on them. Once you're finished, you feel a lot better. You get the piddling work out of the way and are able to enjoy some leisure time. When you're self-employed, you can do what you want to do almost all the time, but if you haven't finished your work, then you don't really enjoy the leisure time and you feel guilty.

I know doctors, therapists, teachers, and other people who have paperwork that goes with their job. A lot of them are procrastinating pros. The situation at one medical clinic in Fargo was so bad that the doctors didn't get their paychecks until their correspondence with insurance companies, finishing charts, etc. was completed. If you are deeply involved in procrastination, it may be the toughest of all hidden handicaps because it is part of so many others. Procrastination has been harder on me than my first six months out of the hospital were. Then I wasn't doing anything, but I wasn't working to pretend I was doing something either. Procrastination is hard work, and you don't want to work hard at something that doesn't pay, so take the easy way out and work hard for the payoff. Harvey McKay says they don't payoff for effort, they payoff for results. But if you don't make the effort, you are not going to get the results. If you understand this, you'll make a change in your life now. There is never a right time to start, so the best time is always right now. Any improvement that you make with this handicap will make your life better and better.

I think when someone is really into procrastination, it's the toughest job in the world. To go all day fooling yourself, your boss, and your fellow workers by appearing to do something and accomplishing practically nothing takes a lot of effort. As I said before, something is usually triggering your procrastination, and you have to identify that something in order to overcome your procrastination. In my case, it's been that I haven't liked what I was doing. So as hard as I've tried to motivate myself or find new goals, it hasn't worked in the long run. Sometimes I have a few months when things go well, and then I'm back in the same rut. In my case, the old saying "if you keep doing the same things, you're going to get the same results" was very apt. That's why I'm taking a chance in writing this book. I'm doing something different, so now I have a chance to get different results. It's risky to change horses in midstream, but that's what you have to do if you're sick of the same old results.

Another hidden handicap that most of us suffer from, the evil sibling of procrastination, is stress. Stress can cause procrastination, but usually it's the other way around. Too much stress usually leads to America's newest epidemic, "burnout." A lot of burnout is caused by the stress of working the same job too long or the stress of working too hard. But a lot of stress is self-inflicted. Two examples of self-inflicted stress are worrying about something that never happens or worrying about something you can't control. Many people worry about things that they think are going to happen. Other people worry about things that have happened that can't be changed. This worry can take on a life of its own. Small worries that aren't controlled or dealt with can become a serious problem. You can worry so much that you start feeling sick. If you do this long enough, you might become unable to perform at your job. Being unable to do your job can cause you to start worrying about getting fired from your job. Even if you don't get fired from your job, you can give yourself ulcers, high blood pressure, headaches, etc. Your worrying then creates new problems, and you start worrying about them and almost forget the original problem.

Stress can also affect you when it doesn't need to if you have a serious problem that has to be settled or solved, but all you do is worry about it instead of taking action. The only thing that is going to solve that problem is action. You can worry forever, and that's not going to solve the problem. But it will cause you stress and make it harder for you to solve the problem.

One of the most effective ways to condition yourself to act on your problems or activities is "blocking out." In sports, blocking out means being able to concentrate on the game itself and not allowing yourself to be distracted by the crowd or the importance of winning the game. When you block out distractions, it allows you to not worry so that you can do your best job of playing the game. I used this technique in golf before my accident. I used to play with a group of seven or eight players at a time. These golf games were played for very big money, and yet there was wisecracking and sarcasm throughout the match. Somebody was always talking when I'd hit my tee shot, and I'd have to block out those distractions.

Blocking out helped me to play golf for high stakes without choking on shots or putts because of the amount of money on the line. I was considered to be the best money putter in our area. There were probably some people who could putt as good in practice, but not as good when under pressure to make the putt. I could block out the pressure mostly because playing almost every sport through grade school, high school, and college helped me to play as well under pressure as I would play with no pressure. Blocking out improves with practice, and I had more practice than others with blocking out distractions.

On the other hand, when it came to blocking out everyday life problems, I was not as good before my accident as I became afterward. It's not so much that I would fold under business and personal problems; it's that I would worry, get very angry, and not handle problems as efficiently as possible. After my accident, I had so many problems, I had to perfect blocking out health, personal, and business problems. I have become better and better at it, and at the present time, I am excellent at the technique of blocking out. My brother Pat, a college administrator and a low-handicap golfer, has told me that he has become much better at blocking out by observing me and talking to me about it. He uses it on the golf course, but he says it has helped him more in his job and personal life. He told me, "I used to think I had to solve a problem right away to get it off my list, even though the timing may not have been the best. Now I can block out the problem and deal with it when the circumstances are better."

My formula for blocking out and reducing stress is quite simple. When I have medical, personal, or business problems, I make a list of what I need to do to solve them. Each day I do all the things I can to address my problems, and then I don't think about them anymore. I can then work on job-related duties, personal duties, or socializing. I've learned to do this because it doesn't do any good to worry. In fact, the stress of worrying does harm to your mind and body. The only thing that helps is action. Do what you can each day, and then stop worrying about the problem until it's time to take action again. During periods of time when there is no action to be taken, which could be two or three days or longer, you must develop patience and control your thoughts so that you don't worry because, again, the worrying is going to accomplish nothing except cause you stress until you reach the point of becoming physically and mentally sick. If you have a job, work hard at it. That will do you some good because you'll be making money, and one way or the other many problems involve money. If you are married, take your family someplace – a movie, out to eat, a sporting event, or whatever it is you like to do. If you're not married, find a friend or do something by yourself. Keep busy until the next time you can take action to solve your problem. Work as hard at solving your problem as you can, do as much as you can, and when there is nothing to do for awhile, stay busy and don't worry. You must convince yourself that worrying accomplishes nothing positive and only makes problems bigger.

Perfectionism is another very frustrating and time-consuming hidden handicap. I have had this handicap for years, and I know how bad it is. In high school and college, I took a lot of accounting classes. Then I realized I did not want to be an accountant, but some damage had already been done. For the fifty years that I have had a checkbook, I have always had to balance it to the penny. It wasn't so bad when I only had one checkbook, but when I got into business, I started having two checkbooks then three; and now I have six. This may seem ridiculous, but I need them all because I use them for my bookkeeping. Most of the time, the girl who I have trained to balance them will balance each book in fifteen to forty-five minutes depending on which checkbook she is balancing. However, there are times when she will spend an hour and a half and then ask for my help, and we might use up a couple of hours trying to find sixty-eight cents or $1.90. On about five occasions, I have found that the bank has made a mistake. I think the longest it has ever taken me to get a checkbook balanced was about six hours. This can be a ridiculous and unnecessary waste of time.

There are many other areas where perfectionism has caused my attendant and me a lot of stress, such as filling out insurance applications or any other applications. Two insurance companies have used my applications for examples on how to fill out an application. When I first went into the insurance business in 1964, I made a trip into the home office of Mutual Benefit Life. We were there for school to learn product knowledge and to see the inner workings of the home office. One day I went out to lunch with an underwriter. He told me how important it was to turn in nice looking applications with all of the questions answered correctly. He said that he and all the other underwriters would take applications that were incomplete with sloppy writing and put them off to the side. These applications would take a lot longer to get processed and issued, whereas the neat ones would fly through in a day or two. It is true that my applications were always issued faster than anyone's in the agency that I was with. If I would have done my applications reasonably well instead of perfectly, I probably would have achieved the same results. I drove myself crazy with concern over properly filling out the applications, but it was even harder on the attendants/ secretaries who worked for me. That is why I always got along much better with the attendants who didn't make many mistakes and/or were perfectionists also.

When you can't do things for yourself, you have to let some of that perfectionism go. But I should have let a lot more of it go. I am much better, but I have a long way to go to be perfect about non-perfect work. For all of you perfectionists, you have to substitute another word for perfection that also starts with the letter "p." The word is progress. You could get so much more done in the same amount of time if you let go of perfection and concentrate on progress. You could also stop swallowing Tums by the handful.

While we all probably realize how difficult procrastination, stress, and perfectionism can make our lives, I wonder how many of us think about the destructive nature hate plays in our lives. Hate is a very destructive hidden handicap. There is too much hate in the world, whether it is one person killing another person, one group killing another group, or full-blown wars. If you take a look at hate, there is always one constant factor: there is never a winner. A lot of hate starts when children are young and their parents teach them to hate a group of people or sometimes objects, towns, or countries. I imagine hate will be with us until the end of time, but if you learn to overcome it in your own life you will be a much happier person.

One way to help you overcome hate is to realize that often the person you hate does not even realize that you hate them. I have seen people literally destroy their lives by being obsessed with hate. Let's take an example where Jim hates his boss George. George did something to make Jim mad. Instead of talking about it with George, Jim starts to hate George. Jim likes his job and gets paid well, so he continues to stay. He is miserable, and George doesn't even know there is a problem. The solution in all cases is to talk to the other person the minute there is a problem. If Jim had talked with George, he might have found out that George did not realize what he had done or if he did realize what he had done, George might apologize to Jim and not do it again. If George is a smart boss, he wants his employees to be happy. When the situation is talked about immediately and not left to grow and take on a life of its own, the problem gets solved and both Jim and George are winners.

What happens if after talking, the problem is not solved easily? Jim still feels better because he got it off of his chest, and both of them have to make a decision so that they can find some common ground. If George is so stubborn that he will ruin an employee rather than admit he is wrong, then Jim may have to find another job. No matter what the result, communicating about a problem is always the best avenue. You owe it to yourself to find out what is going on right away instead of worrying about it for days and days. Most of the time, it is not nearly as serious as you believe it to be.

I have another solution for hate that has worked well for me. It may not be as good as forgive and forget; but sometimes you can forgive, and the other person does not want to forget, so further contact with that person will still be unpleasant. Or maybe the person won't talk to you about the problem. Then my solution is that they don't exist anymore in my mind. I don't wish them any good luck, nor do I wish them any bad luck because no matter what happens to them it doesn't affect me. If they become multimillionaires, I don't care because it doesn't affect me. They have already cost me money or another unpleasantness. I am not going to let them cause me any more stress. It is as if they have disappeared from the earth. I have about three or four people I feel that way about today. I don't discuss them with anybody, nor do I try and find out what is going on in their lives. Use my way, or figure out your own way, but don't hate anyone. It is too destructive for you.

Just as procrastination, stress, perfectionism and hate can be hidden handicaps, physical disabilities can also be hidden handicaps. A friend of mine worked at a college cafeteria for about twenty years. Most of that time, she had terrible pain in both of her feet. Many doctors examined her, but no one could seem to find out what was wrong. She worked about four to five hours a day, and almost every minute was spent on her feet. The pain was nearly unbearable, but she didn't tell her co-workers. So not only was she suffering, but she was also getting no support or admiration for the heroic feat she was performing everyday. Here again, those of us with visible physical disabilities get recognition and praise for all that we accomplish. These compliments are nice to get, and I certainly don't feel they are undeserved; however, sometimes when I get compliments, I feel bad for those of you who are suffering in the dark.

Hidden handicaps are a part of everyone's life and can be devastating. Most people have more than one hidden handicap, and frequently these hidden handicaps build upon or create others or are caused by physical disabilities. Although I've touched on some fairly common hidden handicaps here, there are several other types of hidden handicaps. Before I discuss the stages of hidden handicaps and how you overcome them, I want to share a couple of examples from other individuals who have shared their powerful stories with me. If you haven't identified with a hidden handicap touched on in this chapter, you probably will identify with one in the next chapter.

Chapter 5

HIDDEN HANDICAPS
FROM THE HORSE'S MOUTH

You've heard about a lot of my hidden handicaps. This chapter has other people talking about how their hidden handicaps have affected their lives and how they've dealt with or continue to deal with them. A lot of these stories are difficult, and it took courage for people to share them. They chose to share them in the hopes that their stories would somehow help you either to recognize your hidden handicap or to discover a way to deal with it. That's my hope too.

Dave Schellhase – Recovering from Alcoholism

It was 1985, and I had just been fired from my position as head basketball coach at Indiana State. They told me if I would go to treatment, they would keep me on another year in a different capacity. The officials at Indiana State took me to a treatment center in St. Louis. It was evening, and I was brought to my room. Treatment was to start the next day. There was a book in the room about alcoholism, and, having nothing better to do, I read it. After reading the book, I realized I was an alcoholic. I had been in denial for more than twenty years. I knew I drank a lot, but I never thought I had a drinking problem. I thought that alcohol was a solution. Spending twenty-eight days in the recovery program showed me what a serious problem I had. After I got out of treatment, I spent one year at Indiana State in the office of Development and Public Affairs.

My name is Dave Schellhase. I was a star high school basketball player at Evansville, Indiana. In 1962, I was the leading scorer in the state, and I made the All-State team. I drank experimentally in high school and always enjoyed it. But because of basketball and academics, I didn't have a lot of time to drink. In 1962, I enrolled at Purdue University on a basketball scholarship. In college, I mostly drank beer. I enjoyed drinking, but because of all my commitments, I still really didn't have the time to drink a lot. I made the All Big-Ten First Team in 1964, 1965, and 1966. I was also All-American First Team in 1965 and 1966. In 1966, I was the leading scorer in the nation. I was also a serious student and made the All-Academic Big-Ten First Team in 1964, 1965, and 1966. In 1965 and 1966, I was also All-Academic All-American First Team. I achieved many other honors too numerous to mention. I bring up all these honors to show that I was heavily involved in basketball and very committed to academics. I had a very promising career. My drinking changed all that.

After graduation, the Chicago Bulls of the NBA drafted me as their first-round choice, and I played for them for two years. At this point, my drinking really accelerated. I had a lot of free time, and liquor was available everywhere from locker rooms to airplanes. After games, we hit the bars. No one saw my drinking as a problem, including me.

Once my NBA career ended, I met Wendy, my wife to be, in Chicago. I went back to Purdue University to get my M.S. in physical education, and Wendy and I got married. While in graduate school, I was a graduate assistant for the basketball program under head coach George King. I graduated in 1972 and got a job as a basketball coach for a high school in Frankfort, Indiana. A year later, I became an assistant basketball coach for Marv Skaar at North Dakota State University. I was happy about how quickly my career was advancing. However, drinking was widely accepted in Fargo, so my drinking began to accelerate again. This time I had the reputation of being a drinker. My drinking started to become a problem in my personal life and caused many arguments between my wife and me. However, I blamed all the arguments on my wife. I felt that she was just nagging me without good reason. As I know now, denial is a major part of the disease of alcoholism, and I certainly did not think that I had a problem.

Despite my drinking, my career kept advancing, and in 1975, I became the head coach at Moorhead State University in Moorhead, Minnesota. Moorhead is just across the river from Fargo, so I really did not move anyplace, nor did I quit drinking. My basketball team was doing well at Moorhead State, so I didn't think my drinking was hurting me. But it was affecting my home life and my work performance much more than I realized. I got in an altercation with the police one night, and it made the local newspaper and local television news. This was very embarrassing for me, my family, the people at Moorhead State, and all the Moorhead State fans. Still, I brushed that incident off as nothing very serious. I figured that I had everything under control since I was having a successful coaching career at Moorhead State—our team got into the National NAIA tournament in Kansas City, Missouri in 1980 and 1982. In 1982, I got the head basketball coaching position at Indiana State University in Terre Haute, Indiana. I had achieved my goal of becoming a division-one basketball coach. This was not to last.

My reputation of being a drinker preceded me at Indiana State, and the people there didn't want their coach drinking. I stayed out of bars in Terre Haute because people were watching me, but I started losing control of my drinking. I went to a high school basketball game one night and told my wife I would be home by eleven. At two in the morning, I was drunk and had my first blackout experience. After this, I would hear people say that I was a pretty good coach but that I drank too much. Alcoholism was beginning to handicap me. Things like work, returning phone calls, and personal hygiene weren't getting done. I felt a lack of energy, and I was starting to lie to my family and friends about how much I was drinking. Just as I reached my career goal, my drinking took it away from me. I suddenly became a former head coach of a division-one basketball team in a treatment center. If I had recognized this hidden handicap earlier and listened to the people around me, I would not have lost that job.

After I got out of treatment, I worked one more year at Indiana State, which they had promised me if I would go into treatment. During that time, I started looking for another college basketball coaching job, but it was hard to find. In August of 1987, Ross Fortier, the Athletic Director at Moorhead State University, decided to take a chance on me. I had worked for Ross as head basketball coach from 1975 to 1982 at Moorhead State University before getting the job at Indiana State University. I will always be grateful to Ross for giving me a second chance. Marv Skaar, Head Coach at North Dakota State, who brought me to NDSU in 1973, also had a hand in my coming back to Moorhead State. I also thank Marv for his help. I coached at Moorhead State from 1987 to 1999. I had a contract at Moorhead State that ran out in 1999, and since Ross Fortier left several years before that, the new athletic director did not renew my contract.

For the next year, I coached a professional basketball team in Fargo-Moorhead called the Fargo-Moorhead Beez. I had a lot of fun, but I wanted to go back and get a job near my hometown of Evansville where my parents still live. I took early retirement from Minnesota for the years that I had spent coaching at Moorhead State University. Because of that income, I was able to take a job at a high school forty-five miles from Evansville in a town called Cannelton. It is a very nice town on the Ohio River. I like my job and the people that I'm working with. It's also nice to be close to my parents.

I have been a recovering alcoholic for more than sixteen years, and I'm happy with my life now. I hope I've been a good role model for the kids I have coached since I've stopped drinking. I don't preach to them, but I let them know that I am a recovering alcoholic. I've turned my hidden handicap into a positive thing. My health is excellent, and I feel good about myself. Since coming out of treatment, my family life and professional life have been much better. Sometimes I do think about where I'd be if I hadn't had a drinking problem, but you can't change the past, so that's just wishful thinking.

One woman's story of her hidden handicap – Grief

My husband and I have been friends with Tom Day for many years. I remember when Tom had his accident in July of 1977. My husband and I felt really bad for him and his family. Since his accident, *we have tried to always be there for him when we can.*

It was October of the same year that Tom had his accident that our family's life changed forever. It was the night of a football game between Shanley and North Fargo. Our son was excited to go, as he was home from college at Wahpeton School of Science. The last time I saw him alive was at that football game. The next morning, we received a call from St. Luke's Hospital. A priest called and our second oldest son answered the phone, he looked very nervous. The priest made us aware that there had been an accident and that he wanted us to come to the hospital. The drive seemed like it took forever. When we arrived, I don't remember much, but we were taken into a room where our oldest son was lying. He was about as white as a sheet of paper, but he looked like himself other than a large black and blue bruise on his head. I touched his hand, and it was full of mud. At that point, the shock set in, and I couldn't move. They had found him in a field. Evidently, he had lost control of his car. I think the tire blew, and they rolled and rolled.

I don't really remember much about driving home, but I was thinking about how to tell my children. When we told everyone, my daughter said she thought it was just all a bad dream, and that is how it seemed. Like a bad dream!

Somehow I got through the funeral. I was like a zombie. Nothing seemed real; it was like I was wandering around in the clouds. The first day I was back at work, a lady came in to order flowers for a funeral, and I didn't have the strength to help her. Everyone at work was very helpful, especially Jack Shotwell. This feeling of wandering through life lasted about six months. Then, I woke up one day and realized that he was really never coming back home. After I realized that my son was never coming back, things got really tough.

My husband and I struggled through this period. We weren't able to get together and deal with what had happened. It took five years before we even felt like we were living again. My oldest daughter was severely affected by the accident. As a matter of fact, I believe it changed her whole life and my second oldest son's too. It was really hard on my second oldest son losing his older brother. Our second oldest son was a senior in high school at this time, and his older brother came home to see all of his football games. The older brother had never had a great interest in sports himself, but he was very proud of his younger brother. After the time of our son's death, our whole family suffered the after effects. Our second oldest son began to drink and do drugs, and our oldest daughter became suicidal. Our second oldest son and oldest daughter went to counseling for awhile. I think it helped them, but it still took a long time for them to feel better. We had another daughter who was nine and a son who was eleven. We all suffered, and it was hard for me to help all of the children with their pain, as I was dealing with my pain also. I think it took our oldest daughter until she was married to actually feel she was happy again.

To give you an example of how my son's death continues to affect me, I'll tell you this story. On January 23, 1993, I was going out to my son's grave to put flowers on it. His birthday was on the 27th, and I always go out there sometime during January. I was thinking of him on the way to the cemetery, and I made a left turn when I didn't have the right of way. I hit another car. No one was hurt, but this is an example of what Tom calls a "hidden handicap."

To this day, our family still suffers from the scars of our son's death. We continue to go on, because we have to. But there is a void that only he can fill. There are times that something will remind us of him, and even though those moments are tough, they are getting better with time. We miss him at all family events and pray that he is there with us in spirit.

Lee Gorne – Living with Cancer

I had been experiencing upper back pain for quite awhile. In 1986, it finally got so bad that I went to a doctor to see what was wrong. The doctor did some tests on me but couldn't find anything wrong. He decided to do a whole series of additional tests. When the tests were finished, I went to the doctor to get the results. The doctor said, "I hate to tell you this, but you have cancer. It is called multiple-melanoma. It attacks the plasma cells and the bones. This cancer is incurable. You are in the second of three stages, and you have approximately two to four years to live." I felt so overwhelmed I didn't even say anything. On the way home, I didn't talk to my wife. I was trying to sort out the information that I had just received. The first thing I did when we got home was call the Cancer Society, and they verified what the doctor had said. That first night I didn't get any sleep. I kept thinking, "I have never been ill, and now I'm going to die from cancer." I also thought, "This is going to affect the entire family." I cried, I was angry, and I talked to the Lord. I was having a hard time coping. The next morning I began going through my financial affairs so that it would be easier for my wife and family to go through them once I died. I was still in disbelief and called the Cancer Society again to make sure I was not dreaming. I asked them again how long I had to live, and they said about two to four years.

I didn't go to work for a week, and I struggled with how to tell my co-workers and friends that I had cancer. When I went back to work as an assistant transportation engineer for the State of California, I would be working on a project and temporarily forget about my cancer. Then I would feel the pain of the cancer attacking my bones and be reminded again of my illness. I was unsure if I should pray that the cancer would go quickly or slowly through my body. I wanted more time with my family and friends, but I did not want to suffer the pain or have people take care of me. I finally decided I wanted to live as long as possible and asked the Lord to give me fifteen more years.

The chemotherapy, regular doctor visits to get blood work, prescriptions, and new tests, all kept reminding me of my plight. I realized that if I did not start going places and seeing things I wanted to see, I would not have the chance to do so in my lifetime. My wife and I started going places with the thought of my cancer in the back of our minds. We never could fully enjoy what we were doing. I can no longer drink beer with my pizza or wine with my dinner, as I had to stay away from all alcoholic beverages. I also had to stop eating some of my favorite foods.

At first things didn't seem to be going very well because my tests were coming back very bad. I was taking chemotherapy and all kinds of drugs, and I wasn't getting results with any of them. I got real depressed again and thought that I was on schedule for the two to four years of life. However, then I went into remission, and from 1989 to 1991, I went without treating my cancer. This lifted me out of my depression because I had made it past the four-year mark. I now had a different outlook on life. My attitude changed from being scared, complaining, and uptight to more of an optimistic look on life. I thought, "There are people out there who are worse off than I am, so I should have a different outlook on life." I also starting thinking, "Maybe I can beat this cancer."

I was able to do more traveling, but I knew the cancer was still there because I was not able to do the physical things I was once able to do. People would look at me and say, "You look great." Cancer and many other diseases attack people from the inside and don't really show from the outside. I have had years of radiation and hard chemotherapy, so I know that it is a hard thing to live with. I use one of my best friends since my high school days, Tom Day, as a model for me to get through each day. I figure that if Tom can cope with being a quadriplegic, I can cope with cancer. Tom and I talk on the phone several times a month.

I worked from 1986 to 1994, eight years and ten months. I was able to work twice as long as they predicted I would live. In 1993, I went to my 40th class reunion. My wife Loraine and I really had a good time. It was fun to see all my old classmates, many of them I had been able to keep in contact with by email. I also stopped to see Tom Day during this trip. It was the first time that I had seen him since he had his accident in 1977. For a person paralyzed from the neck down, he amazed me with his attitude.

I had been in remission for several years and had been feeling pretty good. But on the way home in the airplane, when I was placing my luggage in the overhead compartments, my ribs started breaking. When I got off the plane, I had broken ribs on both sides of my body, so I knew I was no longer free from chemotherapy. I was reminded that I was not cured and had only been in remission. The doctor put me back on chemotherapy, but this time I was able to take it in pill form. I continued to take chemotherapy from 1993 to 1995. The side effects were worse then compared to now, and they made me very sick to my stomach. I was also going in for radiation therapy on my ribs, shoulders, thighs, and buttocks to prevent the cancer from attacking those bones. The radiation caused me to be very tired, and I had difficulty coping with everyday life.

In 1995, Loraine noticed that one of my legs was larger than the other one. I found out that I had a blood clot in my upper thigh. It was so large that it had blocked the entire vein. They had to rush me to the hospital for surgery; it was a matter of life and death. I got over the blood clot, and I have been on blood thinners ever since 1995.

In 1996, I had more bone pain, so I had to go back in for additional radiation. In 1996, I was also told that I could no longer take chemotherapy because it would not bring my M protein down; the count had climbed up to 4300. A normal M protein count is around 1500. The doctor now put me on steroids, which was the worst thing I had tried yet. They affected my whole body to the point that my nerves were shot. I had tingling all over my hands and feet. I thought, "Is this how I want to spend the rest of my life, fighting cancer feeling like this? I am on a drug that doesn't permit me to go anywhere, not even out to dinner, because of the way it acts." I stayed on the steroids for six months, and then I said, "No more."

About a week later, I was leaning over the toilet, and my head snapped. I thought I had broken my neck. I had to hold my neck with a towel, and I was taken to the hospital in an ambulance. At the hospital, they took X-rays and found out that the cancer had attacked the third vertebra and had created permanent damage that almost eliminated the vertebra. I was on liquid morphine twenty-four hours a day. The doctors did not think I would live. My head was swollen, and the doctors told me I would be fortunate to make it another day or two. But they were wrong again. After about a week of being in the hospital, they started taking me down to the radiation room. Because of trying to kill the cancer in that area, the radiation killed my saliva gland. This makes it difficult for me to speak without drinking some liquid.

I could not move my head from left to right. I was at home in bed for three months and had to have healthcare nurses come in every day to take care of me. I never felt that I would just as soon die because I figured I had been revived at least three times by the Lord when I should have been taken. However, I did want it to happen quickly when it was my time to go.

After three months, I started walking in my home to try to gain some strength. But I was cramping everywhere. One day, I looked on the Internet for information about my cancer and found a man who was taking thalidomide, and he had had this same cancer for two years longer than I had. I went to my doctor and told him I wanted to try thalidomide because nothing else had been working. So my doctor put me on thalidomide. My M protein was up to 4600 and began to slowly drop. After eight months on thalidomide, I was able to get my M proteins down to 1600, and I felt much better. The thalidomide's down side was nerve damage. My feet, toes, hands, and fingers began to lose all of their feeling. Now I had to make a choice. Did I continue with this drug that could control the main thrust of the cancer, or did I stop because of the side effects? I decided to continue.

Sometimes I think so much about my own problems that I forget about my family and friends. They are all pulling for me because they want me to be around for as long as I can be. Thinking of this helps give me a more optimistic look at life. Still, I would rather not go back to the hospital. I've decided that I would like to die at home. The only time I would go back to the hospital is if I got so bad that my wife and nurses couldn't handle it anymore.

I missed being able to go to my 45th class reunion. I would like to make it to my 50th, but I'm not sure I'll be able to in my condition. At one time, my feet were so swollen and sore from the thalidomide that I had to move around in a wheelchair. Now the swelling has gone down, and I can walk around the house and even walk outside for short distances. I had been feeling really bad for the past six months, but now I'm feeling pretty good again. I still have a lot of pain in my bones, and the morphine only takes the edge off, but it's something I've gotten used to.

I've had a lot of ups and downs, and there were many times when I thought I was going to die, but then things would turn around, and I would get better. I was more depressed the first four years because I was waiting to die. Now that I've made it more than sixteen years, I figure every day is a bonus, and I'm not nearly as depressed. I enjoy my wife, children, and grandchildren, and that makes life worth living.

One woman's story of her hidden handicap – Date Rape

Many years and nights ago, I was date raped. I've been carrying this story around with me for a long time without really telling anyone how it affected me. I've told a few people that it happened, I've even told a few people what I did afterward, but I've only told one person how I really felt about it. Tom's told me that it would help me to write about it and that it would help a lot of other people to hear it. I'm hoping he's right, but it scares me to start writing this story.

I was having a great time. I couldn't believe how much fun John was. Unlike my first boyfriend, he was very romantic. The first time he asked me out, he called and asked if I wanted to take an ice-cream study break. He knew I was stressed studying for finals and thought I could use the diversion. I thought it was a very sweet idea and couldn't turn it down. The next time he asked me out, he showed up with flowers. I had never dated a romantic guy before and was quite charmed. He brought me flowers several more times during the next three months. He also took me out to dinner and dancing. I love to dance, and I couldn't believe he liked it too. I haven't known a lot of men who have enjoyed it and who are good at it. I started thinking, "This could be the one." His southern accent and gentleman manners enticed me as well.

One summer night, he took me to dinner, out dancing, and back to his place. He put on some soft music, opened the sliding-glass door so we could hear the rain falling, and started slow dancing with me. One of my favorite songs came on, and I sang it softly in his ear. He told me he loved me. We must have danced and whispered back and forth for almost an hour. Then he offered to give me a back massage and convinced me that it would be better if I didn't have my clothes on. We had been dating for about three months and had fooled around some, so this wasn't too uncomfortable. Before he started massaging me, he said, "Tonight you're not going to be able to tell me no." I said, "I'm sorry, but I just can't do that." He replied, "Yes, you can. Just wait and see. You won't be able to say no." We went back and forth a couple of times, and then he began massaging me. When he was done, he covered me with his body. I could feel him breathing in rhythm with me.

Then he started moving against me. I got uncomfortable and tried to move away from him, but he grabbed me and held me down. I tried to crawl away and started crying and saying no. He didn't listen. When he was done, he apologized. I got dressed and asked him to take me home. He wouldn't. Instead, he made me go to his bed with him. I said I wanted to sleep on the couch, but he wouldn't let me. He kept saying he was sorry and tried to cuddle with me in bed. As soon as he fell asleep, I went out to the couch and wept silently.

I stayed up all night long trying to figure out what I was going to do. I wanted to get out of there, but that would mean walking home at least three miles through the city at two in the morning. I was too afraid of what else might happen to do that. I was also too scared to call any of my friends or even a cab because I was afraid that if I spoke, he would wake up. My thoughts just kept racing in meaningless circles. I also started thinking that I was never going to be sexually normal again. I had read about women who were raped who no longer wanted or enjoyed having sex. I didn't want that to be me. I think being trapped and fearing that he had ruined me for the rest of my life led me to do something that even I can't really comprehend. Somehow, I got it in my head that if I had sex with him willingly, it would fix everything. I kept thinking that if you fall off a horse, you're supposed to get back on. The next morning, I went back into the bedroom and told him that I wanted to have sex with him. He was very surprised. But he didn't refuse.

I've since learned that having sex with him the next morning was an act of denial. So was dating him for six more months. However, that act of denial has caused me even more shame than the rape itself. I've been told by sexual abuse counselors that that kind of response is normal. Some women marry the men who date rape them, some women become promiscuous with other men, and other women quit having sex altogether. All of these responses are coping devices and are normal responses to being raped. Although I know that intellectually, I can't quite get myself to believe it. I think that's why I can't talk about what happened to me very easily. I judge myself pretty harshly for my response, and I'm afraid others will as well. We all know how the victim frequently ends up on trial. This is true even if others aren't doing the judging. One of the ways I'm trying to get over judging myself so harshly is to think of myself as I would one of my friends. If this were their story, I certainly wouldn't be judging them. I would have great compassion for them, and probably even pity. Somehow it's hard to have that same compassion for myself.

When Tom asked me to write this story, he said that I should be able to do it because I've been working on overcoming this hidden handicap. However, that's not quite true. Yes, I'm working on it (I'm seeing a counselor and going to group therapy), but I also have a lot of resistance. Since this happened to me, I've had a lot of trouble trusting the men in my life. Writing this and thinking about how this hidden handicap has influenced my life and relationships has made me aware of something really important. I've denied how much the rape has affected my life. I thought that the rape wasn't really affecting me because I haven't had trouble having sex and enjoying it. Apparently, I met my goal that morning. However, since the rape, I've never waited longer than three months to have sex with the men I've dated. I used to tell myself that three months was just my breaking point, but that's not true. The truth is that three months is when I no longer trust that men will respect my "no." My relationships with men have always started deteriorating after I've had sex with them. I now understand why. How can I have an intimate, trusting relationship with a man, if I'm having sex with him so that he won't rape me?

As you can see, denying the importance of the rape hasn't kept it from affecting my relationships. In fact, it's affected them in more ways than I had understood, or probably even still understand. I hate to say that because I hate to admit how much he hurt me. But not admitting he hurt me doesn't make the pain go away. Maybe identifying one way it has affected my relationships and breaking that pattern will help the pain die. I'm sure that understanding this pattern gives me a better chance of learning to trust men than if I just keep following that pattern of trying to prevent rape, which is really living that rape over and over again on a subconscious level.

Jim Marshall's Answer to Hidden Handicaps – Thoughts

As most of you know, I played professional football as one of the original Minnesota Vikings from 1961 until I retired in December 1979. I was captain of the Vikings for seventeen of those nineteen years. In November 1999, the Minnesota Vikings retired my #70 Jersey and selected me as a member of the "Minnesota Vikings 40th Anniversary Team." However, my career as a college and professional football star is only part of who I am today. To fully understand the life that I lead, it is necessary to go through a short history that involves key lessons in survival, discrimination, drugs, and the endless search for clear and logical thinking.

I was born on a little farm between Dansville and Parksville, Kentucky. This was a very segregated area. Being a child is a tough enough struggle, but being a black child growing up in this type of environment was very trying and often violent. I remember playing with friends in an open field and having white folks in vehicles shooting at our feet trying to make us dance. I also remember a sign that hung on the edge of a town called Shaker Town that read, "Read Nigger and Run, If You Can't Read, Run Anyhow."

Lucky for me, I was raised knowing my worth since I was taught the confidence needed to learn and to think clearly. I credit my grandfather and father for teaching me many of the lessons I learned early in life. My grandfather would take me into the woods and teach me key lessons for survival. Since he grew up during the Great Depression, he knew that survival meant being able to provide for himself. So he taught me how to make a basket out of branches woven together so that I could catch fish in a stream. He also taught me how to skin animals and use the needles from certain plants to sew them together to make clothes. Rather than teach violence, he taught understanding and knowledge, very powerful weapons.

When I was of school age, my family moved to Columbus, Ohio. The move was a multi-purpose one. My parents moved to hopefully escape the prejudice, segregation, and violence and to secure a chance at a better education for us children. The move was a positive one, but there was still much continued discrimination. For example, in junior high, there were many gangs segregated as blacks and whites. It was important to always travel in groups so that you were never caught alone. In high school, if a black guy was caught dating a white girl, he was subject to brutal violence from the white groups. As time went on, the views started to slowly change, and the ratio of whites to blacks also changed. When I started school, the percentage of whites attending the school was about sixty to seventy percent; by the time I graduated, that number was down to about twenty to thirty percent. This was mostly attributed to the fact that as blacks started moving into the neighborhood, whites would move out by the blocks. Unethical real estate agents bought the houses from the whites at low prices and sold them to the blacks at much higher prices, a term known as "blockbusting." Being in sports throughout high school did help tame some of the violence involved in prejudice. Sports made you popular, and usually if you were popular, you were less of a target.

The biggest question I have about discrimination is . . . why? People of color have to develop a tough skin and learn to process the experiences we have for what they are. My father and grandfather taught me an important lesson to help deal with this throughout the years. They taught that hostility breeds hostility. I used this lesson when people would make prejudicial comments toward me. I would not fuel the fire. I would simply give the person time to wear out. When they were finished and had no more ammunition, I did not reload their gun by returning the hostility. I simply pointed out the logical and the illogical content of the discussion and their differences. I knew to heed my grandfather's advice, which was "never argue with a fool." Lessons like this helped me know that no matter what happens I am always worth something, and when someone makes me feel like I'm not, it is important to process the information coming in for what it is and make a rational decision on how to handle it. Pointing out the truth, facts, and simple logic of others' statements creates an undeniable truth. Most of the time, the attacker is the one with the problem.

As I continued my life as a professional football player, I had many more situations to process. One of these was substance use. When I was in high school, I did not participate in any drug use, as they were always hidden by those who used them and taboo to the non-users. However, drugs became a part of my life in the early 1970's when it was a fashionable pastime. I never really liked drugs because they made me feel out of control, and that was not a feeling I liked. I wasn't addicted to drugs; I just used them to be socially accepted. It was a very foolish way to gain acceptance. Although I wanted to quit, my catalyst for doing so was when I got arrested for possession of drugs in Duluth, Minnesota. I began to understand that I was creating this adverse reality. I needed to understand my relationship with drugs and assess this reality and how it affected my life. I entered a drug rehabilitation center to learn about drugs and their effects and to see if I had the ability to control my substance use.

While I was in treatment, I realized I did not agree with some of the teachings and tactics used to try and help users quit. The treatment center relied on paranoia and fear. I was told I should not associate with friends whom I spent time with when I used to do drugs. That made sense, but to be told not to walk down the streets I traveled when I used drugs did not. I felt that basically this gave drugs an empowerment that I did not believe they had over my life. I believed that I was in charge, not the drugs, and I realized that I was creating the reality that required drugs to be utilized in the equation. After I got out of treatment, I used my own technique, which was to roll two joints, place them by my nightstand, and let them know that I was in control. The joints were helpless to move unless I chose to move them. Later on in life, I used the same technique to quit smoking cigarettes. To this day, I do not do drugs nor smoke cigarettes.

Drinking was never really an issue for me, as it again makes me out of control. I try to do everything in moderation because there are all types of addictions. My lack of interest in drinking is largely due to my college coach Woody Hayes. Woody was a strict disciplinarian, and low achievement in both academics and athletics was simply unacceptable to him. Being a Red One starter as a sophomore, performance was watched very closely. Getting intoxicated was never an option because it could lead to decreased performance. Although I don't drink to get drunk, I do drink socially.

After I retired from professional football, I purchased stock in a small aircraft company that manufactured ultra-light aircrafts. I tried to duplicate the exciting life that I had lived playing professional football and decided to be a test pilot rather than an executive. While test piloting the ultra-light aircrafts, I crashed and spent three-and-a-half years recovering. During those three-and-a-half years, I had a lot of time to think, and I started thinking about how I had been introduced to sports. I belonged to a small group of five kids around fourteen years of age. One day we spotted a beautiful red convertible. I didn't know then that an encounter with the owner would alter the course of my life. We just thought how great it would be to have those beautiful spinner hubcaps on our clubhouse wall. Since I was the fastest member of the gang, I decided I would be the one to steal the hubcaps. Just after sundown, I sneaked up to the red convertible. Using a Cub Scout knife, I began to pry a hubcap from the car, and it began to squeak. I paused for a moment, then resumed. There were a few other squeaks, and then a thunderous voice called out, "Hey! What are you doing?" A giant of a man stood looking at me. I took off like a streak of lightning. Half way down the block, I started to slow down, thinking I was safely ahead of him. Suddenly, a huge hand grabbed me by the shoulder, and for the first time in my life, I was caught. I was very nervous, but the man, in a kind voice, said that I should relax and that he just wanted to talk to me. The man asked me to call the rest of my friends, and I did. He had been observing our gang and commented on how well we worked as a team. He also told us that we were using our talents incorrectly. He said that the worst thing that could happen was for us to continue what we were doing and eventually commit a major crime and go to jail. He asked us if we wanted to use our talents in a more positive way, one that might lead to a more positive life. We answered, "Yes." So he told us to meet him in the morning, and he would give us a ride in his big, red convertible.

The next day, he drove us to Columbus East High School. He introduced us to the coaches and encouraged us to get into a sport we liked. We talked to the coaches and learned how important our grades would be in qualifying to participate in sports. I picked track, football, and swimming. Of the other four, some picked basketball and football, and everyone picked track. After awhile, the man took us home and answered our questions. We wanted to know what was the best and worst case scenario. He told us that if we stayed eligible and participated in a sport, the worst thing that could happen would be that we would get an education. Then he told us the best case scenario, which changed my life forever. He said that if we got good grades and excelled in our chosen sport, we could get a scholarship, go to college, and possibly be picked to play professionally. He told us that we could then live a privileged lifestyle, live in a nice house, have a nice car, money in the bank, and travel all over the world like he did. We must have all been impressed because we all stayed in school, played sports, got good grades, and scholarships to college. The other four members of the gang became an all-pro basketball player for the Indiana Pacers, a college professor, president of the Columbus public school system, and a great all-pro wide receiver for the 49ers and the Rams with a second and third career as a world famous artist and Hollywood actor.

The man who changed our lives was an NFL Hall of Fame Football Player for the Cleveland Browns who started out as an All-American Football Player for Columbus East High School. Later in life, I had an opportunity to thank the man for helping to change the course of my life. I told him that I wished I could pay him back. He responded, "Just pass it on."

That's what I'd like to do right here. From that man, my grandfather, father, and my life experiences, I learned that reality is in our power to create. Our thoughts control our actions, which control our reality. Failure to understand this is perhaps one of the greatest hidden handicaps a person can have because they become victims, trapped and unable to control their experiences. On the other hand, if we recognize our power to control our reality, then we have a very powerful tool for overcoming hidden handicaps. I learned this lesson first from my grandfather and father when they taught me how to deal with discrimination. They taught me to separate myself from the other person's reality. Just because someone is racist does not make their thoughts my reality. I had to understand this in order to keep my self-esteem. I learned this lesson again when the professional football player taught me that my talents could be used productively rather than destructively. My choice on how I was going to use my skills determined my reality. And I learned this lesson yet again when I realized that I controlled the drugs. I could either give them power over me or take control of them. From these examples, I hope you can see how your thoughts determine your actions, and how your actions determine your reality. Once you realize this, you can overcome or deal with any hidden handicap that you have.

Hopefully, these five stories gave you a better understanding of what hidden handicaps are and how they can affect your life. They should also have shown you how taking what most people consider to be the hard way out is actually the easy way out. These stories show that people from all walks of life, races, and both sexes suffer from hidden handicaps. I have one more story that I want to share with you before I talk about my most damaging hidden handicap and how you can overcome yours.

The following story is not about a hidden handicap. This story is about a man who is traveling in the right direction. There are not many people like him. I thought you'd like to hear about a man who almost died or, worse yet, would have been paralyzed with a C-3 cervical break. This is the same spot where Christopher Reeve has his break.

Every year, in the spring and summer, the Spinal Cord Society has a fund drive to raise money for research. The research is to find a way to make quadriplegics and paraplegics walk again. We have a lot of people who have been giving us money for years, and we just call them to renew their pledge. One of these companies was Goldmark. Goldmark is a company that manages and develops property. Every year they gave us $50. In 1999, I called and renewed their $50 pledge. Brad Nordhougen is the chapter head, and the money is sent to his house. He called me up and told me that he had received a $1,000 check from Goldmark instead of the $50 pledge that they had made. Jim Wieland, who neither of us knew, had made out the check. The next year, when I called Jim Wieland, I was careful not to assume that he was going to give us $1,000 again. I thanked him for the $1,000 from last year and asked him what he was going to pledge this year. He said, "Put me down for one thousand again this year." I thanked him very much and said, "We'll have to have lunch one of these days." Jim said, "I'd like to do that. You don't know me, but I know who you are. I see you at basketball games, and we also have a mutual friend in Marv Skaar." We never made it to lunch that year.

In 2001, I called Jim in May or June again and asked him if he was going to give the same pledge. He said he would give at least $1,000 and maybe a little bit more. I asked him to have lunch at the Holiday Inn and said that we could take care of the pledge then. About a week later, we met at the Holiday Inn. After Jim and my attendant sat down and introductions had been made, I said, "Jim, we are very grateful for your donations, but I wonder if you could tell me why you started giving us this much money after giving $50 a year for the past four or five years." The following story is the answer he gave me.

Jim Wieland's Living Gratitude and Generosity

On March 10, 1998, a few friends and I went snowmobiling in Fosston, a small town in northwestern Minnesota. I had a pretty bad cold, so I took some antihistamines to make it easier for me to breathe while wearing a helmet. They must have been pretty strong drugs because I started to doze off while I was on my snowmobile. I veered off the trail and ended up colliding with a tree that must have fallen down during a summer windstorm. My snowmobile went right on under the tree and suffered no damage. My body, however, went through a bit more. My head and upper body hit the tree hard.

My friends were quick to call the Fosston paramedics, and they sent out a team right away. Before they could get there, my friends removed my helmet. I'm lucky that having my helmet removed didn't damage my spinal cord. I was suffering excruciating pain coming from my shoulder, so my friends decided not to move me. That little decision, for whatever reason it was made, probably saved my life. Thank God for small miracles. When the paramedics finally arrived, they stabilized me and put me in the back of a four-wheel-drive pickup to take me to the Fosston Hospital. I don't remember the Fosston Hospital, but I do remember arriving at MeritCare Hospital in Fargo, North Dakota with my shoulder in tremendous pain.

MeritCare was the first place I received any pain medication. That was the good news at MeritCare. The bad news was that the neurosurgeon who could have operated on me was on vacation, so I had to be flown to the Hennepin Trauma Center in Minneapolis, Minnesota. I was flown to Hennepin the next day where their neurosurgeon took a good look at me with x-rays, MRI's, and CAT scans. He informed me that my collision with the tree left me with sixteen broken bones. They included my C-3 vertebrae in my neck, nine bones in my back, my shoulder, some ribs, and a few other various bones, plus a concussion. The neurosurgeon was from south of Valley City, North Dakota. He saw that I was from Jamestown, North Dakota, which is only about forty miles away from Valley City, and he said, "Jim I'm going to take good care of you, and you're going to be all right. You did bruise your spinal cord a little bit, but you're not going to be paralyzed." I really appreciated his words, and I hung on to them. They carried me through the hard days that were ahead of me.

They put on a halo, which really hurt when they screwed it into my head. And then they put on a cast down to my waist to hold the halo and protect the broken bones in my back. I did not move for seven days. Besides my wife and children, I had about forty friends visit me down there. I asked the doctor when I was going to get out of the hospital, and he said, "When you can walk out of here." So that day, I had them sit me up in bed, which was very hard. The eighth day, with the help of four friends, I stood up. The next day I took my first step. On the tenth day, I headed back to the rehab unit at Dakota Hospital. I was riding in a friend's SUV; it was a very difficult and painful ride. When I got to the rehab center at Dakota, there were a lot of friends waiting for me, and I broke down and cried. The trip back and being in Fargo again was a very emotional time for me. The people at Dakota couldn't believe how many friends visited me during the ten days I spent there. At Dakota, they taught me how to walk, get in and out of cars, and all the things I was going to need to do when I got out.

I didn't go back to work for about five months. I was also on narcotic drugs for about five months. The doctor told me that I was addicted to these pain pills but that I needed them because my pain was so severe. After they weaned me off the drugs, I went into a deep depression that lasted for about three months. I went to see a psychiatrist who had come to see me while I was in the hospital, and he helped me a lot. I can understand now people who get hooked on drugs and break into pharmacies to get what they need.

Until I was in the hospital at Dakota, I didn't realize I had so many friends and acquaintances whose lives I had touched. I still run into people at Dakota who call me "The Legend." They said they've never had anyone who's had so many visitors. Before the accident, business always came first. But now if a friend needs help or needs to talk to me, business takes a back seat, and the friend comes first every time. Even though it's been four years since I was hurt, I haven't forgotten how lucky I was, and I still feel I was saved for a reason. I need and want to help people who are less fortunate than I am. I'm back playing golf, and I feel that I've made a complete recovery. I still remember how lucky I am, and I don't ever want to forget that.

I was forty-seven when this happened. I had always appreciated life, but now I appreciated it more. I felt that I was saved for a reason. It was at this time that I realized that I could have been like Christopher Reeve and been on a respirator and a trachea. I had a new appreciation for people like Tom Day and Brad Nordhougen and the Spinal Cord Society. I knew I wanted to help them, and that's why I gave them a $1,000 donation for each of two years and then raised it to $1,500 the third year.

I'm sure you can see the reason why I put this story in the chapter. When most people escape death or a serious disability, they are grateful for awhile, and then they slip back into their same old lifestyle. But not Jim Wieland. I thought it would be nice to give an example of someone who is taking the easy way out. He works hard and plays hard and is living a happy life. Isn't that what we all want—to be happy? If you have some hidden handicaps and work to overcome them, you'll be much happier than you can imagine. A lot of people think they're living a happy life, but that's only because they don't know what real happiness is. I was one of those people. I'm starting to head Jim Wieland's way, and it feels awfully good.

I hope you appreciated these stories. The last one was out of place for hidden handicaps but was so unusual and so nice to see that I wanted to include it. Not many people continue to be thankful when they escape a serious consequence. Some of you have just escaped from something that could have had very serious consequences, but you came out of it all right. Others will have this happen to them in the near future. Remember Jim Wieland's story and continue to be thankful and try to help people who are not as fortunate.

Chapter 6

BEAT THE MASTER AND TAKE THE FRESH

My most destructive hidden handicap was gambling. My father loved to gamble. From the time that my brothers and I were eleven or twelve years old, we were playing poker, Gin Rummy, and betting on sporting events. My father was still playing poker, Gin Rummy, and betting on sports boards when he died at age seventy-seven. However, my father did not have a gambling problem. Some of you may disagree with this, but to my dad, gambling was like playing golf, bowling, or hunting. His leisure time was spent playing cards. My father never played for big money, and he didn't play when there were family obligations to fulfill. In the 1950's and 1960's, my father and his friends played poker with a limit ranging from twenty-five cents up to one dollar. In the 1970's and 1980's, the limit went up to two dollars. My gambling limits started low but escalated. After awhile, it wasn't fun to gamble unless I could win enough money to help me financially or lose enough money to hurt me financially. I gambled for almost fifty years. The first twenty years, I had a small problem with gambling, but the last thirty years were terrible. I did everything the opposite of what my father had done. I lost money that hurt the family, and I missed family obligations when I was gambling.

In high school and college, I played a lot of poker with reasonable limits, and I held my own as far as winning and losing. After college, the limits got higher, and I was losing more than I was winning. I was a good poker player, but I had a problem with not quitting when I knew I should. The smart guys, the guys with control, would win an average amount, and then they would quit. The four years that I took off from college and lived in California, I made a lot of trips to Las Vegas, since it was only two hundred miles away. After I moved back to Fargo, I would continue to go out to Las Vegas four or five times a year. Once in awhile, I would come back a winner, but most of the time, I lost all the money I took with me.

The one form of gambling that I did win money at was golf. Although this winning might seem like it was good, it was actually bad because it led me to believe that I was way ahead in my bets and that, therefore, I didn't really have a gambling problem. I didn't start playing golf until about 1969. A fellow named Duane Albert and I started at about the same time, and we both fell in love with the game. We would play thirty-six holes a day. We didn't take any lessons in the beginning, but we improved pretty fast because we played so much. I shot a par round the first summer I started playing golf. I was a real strong chipper and putter, and that helped me to have good rounds. Duane and I were playing for pretty big money right in the beginning, and most of the time, I would beat him.

My gambling at golf escalated fairly quickly. The first year, I only played at the Moorhead Country Club, where I had become a member. The second year I played, I started playing in big money games at other courses. One day, I lost quite a bit of money in a big game at the Fargo Country Club. The Fargo Country Club was a much tougher course than the Moorhead Country Club. At the Moorhead Country Club, I could get by with slicing the ball and not hitting it very far, but not at the Fargo Country Club. That day, I chipped and one-putted on almost every hole, which is a good thing or I would have lost twice as much money. When I was paying off a friend of mine named Swanny, he told me I had such a good short game that it was a shame that the rest of my game was so lousy. He suggested that I take some time off and take lessons. I took his advice, and for the rest of the summer, I took lessons from the head pro at the Moorhead Country Club, Larry Murphy, who for my money was the best teacher in town. Before the lessons, I had never been able to hook a golf ball, and the distance I hit my woods and irons was not very far. When I got done taking lessons from Larry, I had a pretty good golf swing, and during the next couple of years, my handicap gradually went down from a twelve or thirteen to a four or five.

Although this was good for my golf game, it was bad for my budding gambling problem because it helped me win my bets more often.

In the third and fourth years that I played golf, four of us played at least thirty-six holes a day three to four times a week for big money. The group consisted of Duane Albert, Skip Madsen, Don Halmrast, and myself. Don and Skip were better than Duane and I, so we'd always flip a coin to see if Don or Skip would be Duane's partner, and the other would be mine. We would always have a team bet. In addition, Duane's partner would play him for more money than the team game to protect himself. Also Duane and I would always play each other for enough money that one of us could win $500 to $2,000 a day. I usually won. Duane's problem was that he couldn't play very well under pressure. He also put himself under more pressure by playing everyone in the group for money. Playing under pressure was my strong suit, which came from competing in so many sports all of my life. I was also able to block out the money part of the game. When I was going to putt, I was only thinking of making the putt, not how much the putt was worth. Duane, on the other hand, would go up to a putt, and we would hear him talking about the several bets he had riding on that particular putt and how much the bets totaled. Duane was a great loser. He didn't get mad, and he could laugh at himself.

In addition to winning most of the time, the fact that we were having so much fun kept me from realizing that I was developing a gambling problem. We were laughing almost all the time and gambling was part of the humor. For example, we were playing the number nine hole at Moorhead Country Club, and Duane had about a ten-foot putt that would have won him about $1,000. If he got down in two, he would break even, and if he three putted, he would lose about $1,000. The green was very flat in the area where he was putting. Duane pushed his first putt about five feet to the right of the hole. He was already losing quite a lot of money, so we were all kind of tense while he was putting. After he made that terrible putt, he said that it didn't break. Well of course it didn't break. The green was as flat as a pancake. Skip, Don, and I couldn't help ourselves and started laughing. Duane saw the humor in his remark, and all of us fell on the green and laughed for several minutes. Needless to say, Duane got up and missed the five-foot putt to lose the $1,000.

Another day, the four of us went to a town about sixty miles away, Fergus Falls, to play golf for the whole day. We started at about seven in the morning, played eighteen holes, and had to come back to the clubhouse to pay another eighteen-hole fee and to pay for our carts, as this course did not have an all-day fee like most other courses. We went out and played another eighteen holes and came back to pay our fees again. The pro told us this round was on the house because we had played the most golf he'd ever seen. We played another eighteen holes, so we had fifty-four holes in for the day. When we got done with the last hole, Duane was the only loser. The other three of us had played enough golf for the day, and it was starting to get dark. Duane was a master at keeping any gambling game going when he was behind. So he went over to the first tee stand, teed up his ball, hit it, and yelled at us to keep playing. We yelled, "Duane we've had enough golf for the day." Duane said, "Sure you play a few holes with a guy, get him stuck, and then quit on him." Gambling made golf not only fun, but also funny.

In the last two or three years before I got hurt, the bets would sometimes get up to as much as $1,000 per hole by the end of the round. The team games were also for big money, so between individual bets and team bets, we could easily win or lose $2,000 to $4,000 a day. Most of the time, I came out ahead. When we played golf, we always used carts and would play eighteen holes in two hours, so I still had plenty of time for work. However, I would also play poker two or three times a week. This obviously did not leave much time for me to spend with my family. I was very unfair to my wife and children. Even though I was winning at golf, I was beginning to realize that I had a big gambling problem that was taking time away from work and the family. Also, when I won a lot of money, it seemed to disappear, and when I lost money, it would come right out of my paycheck. Even though I noticed that I had a problem, I didn't quit gambling. It took my accident to put a halt to my gambling on the golf course.

After my accident, it took a couple of years before I started working again. After I did start working, I was making good money, and I began gambling again. Although I couldn't play golf, I could still play poker. So my good friend Tom McCormick and I bought a house and converted it into a four-plex. We rented out three of the apartments and used the fourth one for poker only. I ran a poker game there every Monday night for about fifteen years. There was a period of three or four years when I ran a lot of poker tournaments, and we ran high-limit games. We had players coming from western North Dakota, South Dakota, Iowa, Minnesota, and Wisconsin. Sometimes we would play for three or four days straight. I also had a football pool, and for twenty weeks during the football season, I ran it with forty to fifty members. I was making good money working, but I was losing more than I was winning and spending an awful lot of time away from my family. Just like an alcoholic, a gamble-holic tries to rationalize his behavior. I told myself that I could no longer play golf and participate in the other activities that I did before I got this disability and that since poker was my only activity, I deserved it. Boy, was I fooling myself!

As I said, we had players from all over the Midwest, and a lot of them were excellent poker players and characters. This made the gambling costly, but entertaining for me. The very first tournament that Phil Helmuth played in was one of my tournaments in Fargo. Big Al, who played a lot at our place, brought Phil to the tournament. Several years later, Phil won the World Series of Poker at Binions in Las Vegas. First prize was almost $1,000,000. With inflation and more players, first prize in the World Series of Poker is now $1,500,000. With $2,800,000 in winnings, Phil is now the top money winner and does color commentary in the big tournaments, if he gets knocked out. One of the real characters who often came to our games was Albert Alan Anderson from the Minneapolis area. The first time he told me his name, I gave him the nickname of Triple A. The name stuck, and until his death, he was known as Triple A. Every time Triple A sat down at the poker table, he'd buy his chips and say, "Beat the Master and Take the Fresh." For those of you lucky ones who don't play poker, "master" means that you are the best, and "fresh" is a poker term for money. Another time, Triple A was the big winner and had $4,000 to $5,000 worth of chips in front of him. Two to three hours later, the chips were all gone, and he was buying chips again. Instead of getting mad, he said, "I have proven again that no amount of chips is safe with me." None of us thought that we had a gambling problem. However, as I said, I was beginning to lose more than I won. I was running two to three poker games per week and holding a few tournaments a month, and when I ran a game, I had to stay until the end. It is very hard to stay until everyone leaves and still come out ahead. I wasn't a bad card player, and I think that is what kept me going so long. But even though I knew how to play, many times I played too many hands, and if I got stuck, I went on tilt (played every hand). Another friend of mine named Jack also used to play poker with us. When he was losing, he used to say, "I don't want the cheese, just let me out of the trap." What he meant was that he didn't care about winning any more, he just wanted to get his money back. Unlike Jack, I wanted to get out of the trap with the cheese.

I got so bad that even though I was hurting my kids, especially my son, Mike, I still wouldn't quit. All of my kids held my cards for me at some point, but Mike held them the most. When Mike was growing up, I taught him the value of telling the truth. His Grandpa Day was one of the most honest people in Detroit Lakes, and Mike tried to emulate his grandpa. When Mike was holding my cards for me, I told him to lie to his mother about how much I had lost. Mike and I had big fights about him lying to his mother. He wouldn't do it, and he had the courage to stand up to me. If she asked him, he would tell her the truth, but if she didn't ask, he wouldn't say anything. I had also told Mike when he was younger that he could cheer for any team he liked even if I had money on the other team. Later, as he got older and I was betting more, I would get angry with him for cheering for a team that I had bet against. I also frequently blamed my losing on him. For example, if I lost the pot in a hand of poker, I would blame Mike for throwing the wrong card. I would shout and scream at him in front of his peers. I would do this even though he hadn't thrown the wrong card. I almost destroyed my life, Mike's life, and my relationship with him over gambling. Mike survived because of his loyalty and character and because he understood the sickness enough to know that I wasn't deliberately trying to hurt him. Ironically, he stood up to me because of the values I had taught him when he was young, even though my obsession with gambling was causing me to throw my values out the window. Fortunately, my son had the courage to stick with what I had taught him. He kept telling me that I had a serious problem. But I didn't want to change that yet, so I got a different person to hold my cards, which was fine with Mike and with me. Mike then got a job dealing black jack with the charities so that he wouldn't be around at nights when the games were on, as he lived in the apartment where we played cards. Even though I was beginning to see that I had a problem, I wasn't doing anything about it.

It took a lot for me to quit gambling. In 1994, my wife and I divorced, and she moved out of Fargo. There were a lot of reasons why she left, and gambling was certainly one of them. When she filed for divorce, I quit gambling for awhile. But about six months after Lynda left, I started gambling full time again. In January of 1997, I pretty much decided I was going to quit gambling because of my desire to stay out of a nursing home. I realized that gambling was taking too much time away from working. I was playing poker Monday, Tuesday, and Thursday night, leaving the house at five each night. On top of that, I was going to the casino at least two weekends a month to play in poker tournaments, and about once a month, I would hold a poker tournament. I wanted to stay at home and not go to a nursing home, but gambling was pushing me in the wrong direction. In March 1997, I had a weekly counseling session with Reverend Brunsberg. It was about a twenty-minute drive to his office, and on the way over, I changed my mind about a thousand times. I was going to tell him; I wasn't going to tell him; I was going to tell him; I wasn't going to tell him; and back and forth I went. When I got to his office and Liz (my attendant) closed the door, I blurted out, "Paul, I have a problem with gambling. For the last six or seven years, I have told you the truth about everything else in my life, but I have lied to you about my gambling." We talked for an hour, and he agreed to be my counselor for gambling along with everything else.

I made him a promise that if I even bought a $1 lottery ticket, I would tell him. Since then, I have had some urges to gamble, but it hasn't been as bad as I thought it would be. I filled in the hours I usually spent gambling with time with my kids, grandkids, and working. I also probably go to a few more sporting events now, although I went to an awful lot of events before I quit gambling.

I know how hard it is to give up addictions. No one wants to give up his or her highs. For example, I have known quite a few manic-depressives. Their problem does not come from their own choosing, but from a chemical imbalance that they are born with. However, just like addictions, they have tremendous highs and very dark and depressive lows. Although there is medicine available to even out their moods, when they take this medicine, they don't have the lows, but they also don't have the highs. Some manic-depressives stop taking their medicine because they miss the highs and are willing to suffer the terrible lows to get the highs. We had a girl working for us who was manic-depressive, but neither she nor her parents told us about her problem. We wish that they would have told us, but we understand why they didn't. If we would have known, maybe we could have helped. When this girl started working for us, she had a mellow personality, but after awhile, we started noticing huge mood swings. Unfortunately, we didn't realize that she was manic-depressive. She was tough and worked through her lows, but when she was on her highs, she worked like a white tornado. One Sunday, she said she was going to a sorority dinner and event. She took a shower and got all dressed up. She looked beautiful. We'll never know when she headed out the door if she intended on going to the sorority or if she knew then that she was going to commit suicide. Maybe she changed her mind on the way to the sorority house. Anyway, she didn't come home that night, and the next day we were notified by the police that she had jumped off a water tower to her death. She obviously had stopped taking her medicine, and her mother said that they had had trouble keeping her on it. I think about how exhilarating her highs must have been to suffer through the lows that were so bad that she would take her life. I think that this explains a lot of people with hidden handicaps that keep going and hiding them until it's too late. Although this chapter is about gambling and the paragraph above explains the highs and lows of a manic-depressive, there are many other hidden handicaps that have extreme highs and lows. Some of these are pornography and other perversions, alcoholism, illicit love affairs, rape, and stealing. These and many other hidden handicaps have tremendous lows, and many of them you can go to jail for. But the highs are what keep a person doing these things. You need a lot of help to get over these hidden handicaps.

Although I didn't really realize how bad my problem with gambling was until it threatened to put me in a nursing home, there were signs for me to recognize it much earlier. If I had paid attention to the lows instead of the highs of gambling, I might have taken action before I hurt my family so badly. One of my gambling stories that is sad and humorous at the same time is the Daryl Dawkins story. It's sad because when the team that you are cheering for wins the game, you should be happy, not a raving maniac. Daryl Dawkins played for the Philadelphia 76ers back in the Julius Erving days. I bet $200 on Philadelphia giving five and a half points. For non-gamblers (intelligent people), this means that Philadelphia had to win by six points or more for me to win my bet. Daryl Dawkins got fouled with one second to go in the game and with Philadelphia leading by five points. The rules in the NBA at that time were that he got three free throws to make two. All Daryl had to do was make one free throw out of three attempts. The first shot he shot was underhanded; the second attempt was a Meadowlark Lemon hook shot. Daryl was laughing all the time that he was doing this, and my anger was escalating. I was screaming, "Daryl make the last one!" For the last attempt, Daryl took the ball from the official and closed his eyes. I was screaming, "Dawkins open your eyes!! Dawkins open your eyes!!!" as Dawkins, with his eyes still shut, lofted up a ball that didn't hit the rim. Philly won the game, but I lost my bet by half a point. I went ballistic. The reason I remember this story so well is that my son, Michael, has told it to other people in my presence one thousand, eight hundred and seventy two times. Obviously, there is some humor here, but that's only because my low was so extreme.

I have another tragic but humorous story about sports betting.

In no way are these humorous stories an endorsement of gambling. They are intended to show that the lows of gambling can turn the pleasure of watching an athletic event into a tragedy. As I've said, some people can gamble for small amounts and do it infrequently. They are not out of control. But those of us who spend a lot of time and bet large amounts of money have a serious problem. This friend of mine, we'll call him Bill, had a bet on a game involving Atlanta and another team. I don't remember the exact circumstances, but if the score had remained where it was, he would have won $1,000. On the very last play of the game, the Atlantic quarterback threw a pass to Billy "White Shoes" Johnson that he caught on about the five-yard line and tried to pull himself into the end zone. The referee signaled touchdown, and my friend Bill lost $1,000. This was before the days of instant replay. The television rerun of the play showed that Johnson was at least a yard short of getting into the end zone. Bill was furious. To make matters worse, for the next week or two, that play was shown over and over as an example of why football needed instant replay. Bill said he has seen the rerun twenty-five or thirty times, and he has heard me retell the story about five hundred times. At the time he lost that $1,000, he wasn't making much more than $1,000 a month, so the loss really hurt. That's the thrill of gambling. You have to bet enough so that if you win, it helps your financial situation, but conversely, if you lose, it is going to hurt you financially. It's that loss that can cause the extreme low.

When you have a gambling problem, it is a hard addiction not only to admit, but also to realize that you have. In fact, other addictions such as alcoholism and drug addiction all have similar features. The highs are so good that it takes a long time for the lows to be worse than the highs. Let's zero in on gambling. When you are gambling, you get a lot of rushes. When you win a hand of poker, you get a high, and when you lose a hand, you get a low. But throughout the game, even if you are losing, the anticipation of winning is still there. If you leave the game with a big win, you really feel good, and you have grandiose ideas that next time you will win more. You also think of all the things you can do with your money. This is the same for any type of gambling: craps, blackjack, slot machines, etc.

Now if you leave the game with a big loss, you're depressed. Sometimes you are wondering where you are going to get the money to pay off the loss, if some of it was on credit. You think about not gambling anymore. The next day you come up with a way to pay off the loss, or if you had the money, you start adjusting to the loss. Pretty soon, you're thinking about the next game or trip to the casino and how you are going to win it all back. You start getting a high, and the endorphins are flowing in anticipation of gambling. When you get to the casino, you almost run to the slot machines, the blackjack table, or the crap table. If you're going to play live poker or a poker tournament, you can hardly wait until it gets started. Sometimes you play blackjack or slots while you are waiting for the game to get going. It takes a long time to bottom out if you're a bad loser because you keep coming up with new ideas of where to get the money until you crash.

Many people win one day and lose the next. They go back and forth in their cycle of winning and losing. They think they are about even, but most of the time, they're losing. And even if they are about even, they're losing for this reason: the winnings get spent on things they ordinarily wouldn't buy, but when they lose, it comes out of their checking or savings account or is added to their credit card. Having a gambler with several credit cards that have high limits is like having a fox guard the hen house. The other thing that gamblers don't think about, and it took me a long time to admit this, is the amount of time they spend away from their family. I would never miss any of my kids' extracurricular activities, but I missed plenty more. I missed things such as taking my wife out for dinner and dancing or to movies, plays, concerts, etc. She usually did all of these things with her girlfriends. I also missed out on taking my kids on trips, to movies, and going to parent-teacher conferences. My wife went to nine, and I would go to one. Gamblers do not realize the amount of time their gambling takes away from many important events in their life. They also spend a lot of time with people whom they wouldn't ordinarily do anything else with. The conversations that they have while gambling are usually not very stimulating. There are a lot of gamblers with a take-it-or-leave-it attitude that don't have a problem. They are also not trying to make a living by gambling. They set aside so much money when they go to a casino, and when the money is gone, they're gone. If you gamble at all, which category do you fall into?

I had decided that I had a gambling problem about ten years before I quit. Before I got hurt, I won so much money on the golf course that I figured I was way ahead in gambling. But I wasn't thinking about the time it was taking away from my family, which I can never get back. After I started thinking I had a problem, I would rationalize and convince myself that I didn't, and then the thought that I had a problem would come back into my head, and I would start rationalizing again. I went back and forth like this for close to ten years. I went through a period from 1990 to 1994 of not playing poker because Lynda had demanded that I quit. I didn't play any poker for four years, but I did play a little blackjack and did some sports betting that Lynda didn't know about. When she told me she was filing for divorce, she told me one of the reasons was that I had been gambling again. The truth of the matter is that I wasn't gambling nearly as much as she thought I was, but I did lie to her about not gambling at all. It really didn't make any difference how much or how little I had gambled during that period, as the damage had been done long before that. There are too many stories to even start telling them about me gambling when Lynda needed me at home. Suffice it to say, it happened way too much.

When I was gambling, a person had to be in awfully bad shape for me to think that they had a gambling problem. Since I had the same problem as most of the other gamblers, they all looked normal. Now that I have quit gambling, I look at a lot of these same people and see things that I hadn't seen before. I see people who lost their wives and relationships with their kids because of gambling. I also see a lot of people who don't think they have a problem because they don't lose much gambling or they may even win. But they spend an incredible amount of time gambling. These same people who don't think they have a problem gamble thirty to forty hours a week. They don't necessarily gamble for big money but think of the time they waste that could be spent more constructively. And as if that isn't enough, what do you think they talk about when they are not gambling? You got it, gambling! They also gamble in rooms that are so smoky that even the smokers can't stand it. True story. I asked a friend of mine who smokes close to two packs a day why he wasn't playing in a certain poker game in Minneapolis. He said he couldn't stand the smoke. If he couldn't stand the smoke how could the non-smokers stand it? They must really want to play.

Another reason that made it tough for me to quit gambling was that my dad gambled and had introduced me to gambling. Everyone in Detroit Lakes liked my dad, and he was a respected member of the community. How could gambling be wrong if my dad did it? It took a long time for me to figure out that gambling isn't necessarily wrong. What was wrong was that I was gambling in excess. My father gambled in moderation.

There are a lot of you who have the same problem that I do. You are gamble-holics. The telltale signs are when it hurts your relationships, you lose money you can't afford to lose, and you have to borrow money to pay off losses. You know you have a problem, but you stay in denial. There are times when you know for sure that you have a problem, but then within a couple of days, you have yourself convinced that you can start playing better and controlling your losses. You say you will stop gambling so much, and for awhile you may. But pretty soon, you lose your cool, your money, and you are back in trouble. If you see yourself in my story, don't wait until you are sixty years old to do something about it. Go to a counselor or tell somebody about it now. Even though it took me until I was sixty to talk to a counselor about my gambling problem, the last five years have been the best five years that I have spent with my family. Somehow I now seem to have more time for them and work. I wonder why . . . ?

Chapter 7

OVERCOMING HIDDEN HANDICAPS

To the millions of you suffering from hidden handicaps, I offer my support and admiration for your continued battles with your invisible demons. The question is: "How do you overcome these hidden handicaps?" Well, as I see it, there are four stages of hidden handicaps, each with its own challenge to overcome. The first stage, and perhaps the most dangerous stage of a hidden handicap, is the unknown stage. This stage occurs when you have a hidden handicap, but you do not know that you have it. It's causing problems for you, and you might be aware of the problems, but you don't know what's causing them. With the second stage, the denial stage, you now know you have a hidden handicap, but you deny the extent to which it is affecting your life. In the third stage of a hidden handicap, the resistance stage, you know you have a problem and the extent of the problem, but you either don't want to do anything about it or are afraid to do something about it, and so you won't get help. Finally, the fourth stage is the working stage. In this stage, you have decided to do something about your hidden handicap and are working with a counselor or some other type of professional to eliminate it.

With these four stages in mind, it becomes obvious that the first step in overcoming a hidden handicap is identifying that you have the problem. This is not an easy step. Sometimes you can do this on your own; but more often others or life itself makes you aware of your hidden handicap. In my case, it took a long time for my wife, family, and friends to convince me of some of my addictions and personal problems. In fact, the outside world knew of many of my hidden handicaps before I did. I can guarantee that if the people who love and care about you are telling you that you have a problem, you have one. If no one's told you that you have a problem, but life's events are starting to make you wonder if you have a problem, let's say with drinking, then the simplest course of action would be to act according to your best interests, which would be to stop drinking. If you have difficulty quitting drinking, then it's a problem for you. However, if you have no difficulty quitting and you were wrong about it being a problem for you, you certainly haven't hurt yourself by giving up alcohol. On the other hand, if you do have a problem and you don't quit drinking, the effects could be disastrous.

Once you take the first step and identify your hidden handicap, the next challenge is getting out of the denial stage, which is thinking that the hidden handicap is not *that* big of a problem. I used to have many hidden handicaps in the denial stage. One of my denial-stage hidden handicaps was anger. I could get angry for the smallest of reasons, and it could come on in seconds. I always knew I had a bad temper, but at first I was too proud to admit the extent of my problem. I give my wife, my kids, and my brothers and sister tremendous credit for continuing to love me and staying with me, while trying to make me understand the terrible effects my anger had on them and on me.

My problem with anger coupled with my ability to sell was deadly. From the time I was a youngster, I was always good at selling, and as I got older, I got better. I consider myself a super salesperson. Whenever somebody tried to tell me that I had a problem, they were faced with a tremendous one-two punch. I was a very powerful salesperson with an anger that could scare a mountain lion. They never had a chance. But who was the winner? Not me. I was the loser. I kept getting angry until I lost my wife and almost lost my relationship with my children and my siblings. Because of my anger, I also lost some good employees and made some average employees and girls not suited for the job feel terrible. I had to correct this handicap, or I wasn't going to be able to stay at home. I had to admit that anger was a problem before I could move out of the denial stage.

One of the best ways to move out of the denial stage is to start telling people that you have a problem. I'm hoping that by sharing with you some of my experiences that many of you will be encouraged to talk to someone about problems that you may never have discussed with anyone or that you've only shared with very few people. It's an awfully hard thing to do. But once you talk to someone, you feel some relief, and the healing process begins. After I was injured, I had many hours of counseling to help me adjust to all of my losses. Most of the counselors and psychiatrists were very bright, but they had no idea where I was coming from. Fortunately, the lady in charge of occupational therapy was just like NBA basketball— FANTASTIC! I credit her with helping me find the strength and ability to deal with my losses, which were so extensive that it was a year before I even realized I wasn't smoking anymore. She helped me put my losses in perspective and start the process of overcoming the denial phase.

I really learned how important talking about the problem was to overcoming the denial stage about a year and a half after I was injured. At that time, I wasn't working, and Lynda took care of me a lot of the time. She went to play tennis one day and got her best friend and a good friend of mine, Ann Fortier, to baby-sit me while she was gone. For some reason, I started telling Ann how some of my losses were bothering me. I constantly thought about hugging my wife and kids, and about walking, running, tennis, golf and just about anything else that you do by moving. As I mentioned in the first chapter, my accident happened about three miles from Glyndon, Minnesota. This town is about twelve miles from Fargo, North Dakota, where I live, and about thirty-five miles from Detroit Lakes, Minnesota, where I was coming from. Thousands of times in my mind, I tried to make that drive from Detroit Lakes to Fargo without having an accident. I thought about all the things I could have done to avoid the accident, like not having had that breakfast at one in the morning that made me tired, or maybe having stopped the car and walked around until I felt more alert. But no matter how hard I tried, I never got to Glyndon. But now I'm going to tell you something that seems very basic and somewhat silly, but believe me it worked! After I had talked to Ann in some length about my denial, she said, "Tom I want you to try something." She came over and sat very close to me and talked into my ear. She told me to think about all the good things that I could no longer do. She said to imagine myself hugging my wife and kids, playing golf, and not being paralyzed. She gave me several minutes to do this, and then she screamed in my ear, "STOP!" It scared the hell out of me. She said, "Now Tom, anytime you start thinking about the past and what you can't do anymore, remember my scream." As crazy as it sounds, it worked. Almost immediately I could stop dwelling on the past. And after twenty-three years, I'm about ninety-nine percent effective in not letting the past disrupt my life or depress me. I remember the past, but I don't dwell on it. I no longer use it to deny my present state.

For those of you in denial for whatever reason, I doubt if Ann Fortier will shout in your ear, and even if she did, it probably wouldn't work for you. You'll have to find your own way. If anybody is wondering if they're in denial, remember your problems don't have to be as obvious as mine. Whenever something is causing you stress, affecting your work, and hurting your family relationships, more than likely you recognize the situation but deny that it's a problem. It's not just the alcoholics who have to admit they have a problem. All of us have to admit and then work on our hidden handicaps.

Once you identify that you have a problem and admit the true degree to which it is a problem, the next stage to overcome is the resistance stage. This is when you know you need to do something about the problem, but you don't want to or don't know how to take the necessary action. You may be wondering why anyone wouldn't want to take action if they knew that it would eliminate the problem. It's really not that hard to understand. Take, for example, people who are manic-depressive. Some people are born manic-depressive, and in other people it is triggered by many stresses in their lives. I have a friend named Pete who falls into the last category.

Pete's mother died when he was very young, and his father died soon afterward. When he was in high school, the aunt who was raising him also passed away. After school, Pete went into sales and did very well for himself. He also made some good investments in a number of properties and came out very well when he sold them. He and his wife decided to move their family to California to start a new life. But after a few years, his wife left him for another man. They ended up getting a divorce, which was long and costly. Pete, who was self-employed, was under a lot of stress because of the divorce and because he split half of his estate with his ex-wife and lost the other half through some bad decisions. Pete's stress was even greater because he was self-employed. When you have hidden handicaps, such as the stress of a broken marriage, being self-employed is much more difficult than having a job where you're paid hourly, weekly, or monthly. With that type of job, you can go to work at eight, fight your way through the day, and go home at five. No one knows how badly you are suffering, but you have a place to go every day, and how well you perform under the pressure depends mostly on the amount of skill your job takes. When you are self-employed, like Pete, no one is forcing you to do anything each day. And when you are selling, you need to be creative and positive, and you need a clear mind. Whenever I train salespeople, the most important part of training is to clear their mind. If I don't get them to clear their minds, I can teach them sales psychology and give them product knowledge, but it is going to be almost impossible to motivate them to prospect and sell. In Pete's case, the stress of his divorce led to failure in his sales, which added to his stress. On top of that, he had ten years of alimony and child support, which added more stress. It was at this time that the signs of becoming a manic-depressive hit him.

Pete didn't know what was wrong. He was hospitalized for depression and was being treated for depression only. I remember talking to him back then. One day, he would be trying to get me into a multi-level business telling me he was going to be making ten thousand dollars a week in just a few months. The next time I would talk to him, he would be trying to borrow money and sleeping in his car, and terribly depressed. Because he didn't have any money, he wasn't getting the best medical treatment, and it took several years before they figured out that he was manic-depressive. Once they got him on the right medicine, he became his old self. Now, when I talk to him on the phone, he seems like the Pete I knew before. He told me that when he was in the manic stage, he wasn't living in the real world. He thought he could accomplish anything. Pete's never used drugs, but he figured he was higher than someone on drugs. According to Pete, manic-depressives have to fight the urge to quit taking their medication because even though the medication gets rid of the extreme depression, it also gets rid of the extreme highs. Some manic-depressives go off their medication just so they can get that high again. In some cases, this has been fatal. Once the high wears off, the low is so low that they can sometimes take their own life. So once you identify your problem and acknowledge its negative effects, you have to overcome your resistance to doing something about it and move into the fourth stage, the working stage.

These stages don't always come in order. For example, because of one event in my life, I became aware of my hidden handicap, acknowledged the extent of its damage to my life, and was forced into taking action to correct it, completely skipping the resistance stage altogether. In order to explain to you how I was thrust into the working stage of my hidden handicap, I need to tell the short version of this story. The end, and devastating result for me, is that I lost my North Dakota and Minnesota insurance licenses.

The story starts in 1986, nine years after my accident, when a life insurance agent came to a doctor friend of mine in California and told him that he could give him a million-dollar life insurance policy free. My friend told him that he got all his insurance from me and that the agent would have to talk to me about it. The agent told my friend to have me call him if I had any questions. I called him and found out that the company he was using was Mutual Benefit Life. This is the company I started with in 1964 and left in 1974. I knew some general agents with the company, so I called them to see if this was for real, and I found out that it was. The total commission, with minimum deposit and overrides, was approximately one hundred sixty percent. The agent asked me to help him sell to my friend and to all the other doctors in his clinic and said he would split the commissions with me. One hundred percent of the commissions would make the insurance free for all the doctors, and we would split the sixty percent. He was working for a large agency in Los Angeles and sent me copies of his commission statements showing that they were netting out the commissions on the statement. When I looked into it more, I found out that a lot of other big companies were doing similar things. Their whole life product had been canceled and changed to a new product called universal life. The universal life appeared to be a better product for the policyholder, but the companies didn't get the same tax break on a universal life as they used to get on whole life. So they wanted to put some whole life back on the books. At that time, rebating was legal in California and Florida, so I thought I would make some easy money and that would be it.

In 1987, a general agent in Fargo, whom we'll call George, became involved with a company that paid out one hundred fifty percent commission on a policy to an agent. I had told him what I was doing in California, and he decided to do it in Fargo. He asked me to sell insurance for him. In 1987 and 1988, I sold a lot of this insurance. I used it for my big term clients, and they gave me a lot of referrals. There were also about twenty to twenty-five other agents writing these policies for George. I didn't sell much of this insurance in 1989, and in August I had stopped selling it altogether. Several months later, George had a fight with his office manager, and she turned him into the insurance commissioner.

The nightmare started in January of 1990 when the insurance commissioner's investigators made copies of all the files, commission statements, and checkbooks in George's general agency office. I was investigated along with George, but none of the other agents were ever brought into the investigation. We realized too late that the insurance commissioner was using this investigation and the publicity that went with it for political reasons. If he had brought in the other twenty or more agents involved, rather than just the two of us, it would have looked like everyone was rebating, as we had said. The deputy insurance commissioner asked me on several occasions if there were any other agents involved. He knew very well that there were other agents involved because he had all their commission statements. Many of the other agents involved were friends of mine, and I didn't want to drag them through the hell that George and I were going through. I also realized that it wouldn't help us, so I didn't say anything. I would also like to clarify for the record that my wife, Lynda, was not involved and did not know what I was doing.

In April of 1990, I was charged with rebating, and I voluntarily surrendered my insurance license and paid a $10,000 fine. Rebating is giving the insured customer a discount on their insurance. This is legal in the business world, but is not legal when selling insurance. I still don't think it was immoral, but I certainly knew it was against North Dakota insurance statutes. I knew that I would lose my insurance license if I ever got caught. The rest of the story isn't important to the content of this book. I only mention it for two reasons. The first reason is to explain why my income went down drastically starting in 1990. Prior to 1990, my income averaged $140,000 a year, and since 1990 it has averaged about $70,000 a year. The ridiculous part of this story is that I was making enough money without rebating. It just became an easier way to make about the same amount of money. Again, the easy way turned out to be the hard way. The second reason I tell this story is that the names of all the people who bought insurance and got a rebate were passed around on a list that was made available to anyone who wanted it. These people got taxed on the rebates they received. They should not have been taxed because it's just like getting a rebate on a car, and you don't pay income tax on that. But in this case, the IRS made them pay. I thought I lost a lot of friends because of these circumstances, and recovering from this was harder than when I had my accident. This is when I learned firsthand how hidden handicaps could destroy you even more than physical disabilities because other people don't realize how much you are suffering. I stayed away from many of my friends for awhile and slowly found out that people I thought were angry with me weren't. But I did lose some friends. By now most of these friendships have been repaired. There are only a few people left who are still angry, and I realize now that they were never really good friends.

I continued to realize the devastating effects of hidden handicaps as losing my insurance licenses in the rebating incident affected my emotional and financial life. Not only were we not making the amount of money that Lynda and I had been used to making, but also I was extremely depressed because my friends had to pay taxes on the rebates. This incident caused a whole array of hidden handicaps: depression, financial problems, low self-esteem, and having to try new professions for which I had little or no experience, etc.

Lynda and I tried to solve our financial problems by selling some of our assets, which was a big mistake that hurt us emotionally and financially. We had a house on the river that we were renting out until we could sell the house we were living in. Instead of selling the house we were living in, we sold the house on the river in a bad market and lost $20,000. In 1991 in order to make ends meet, we sold some lakeshore property at Detroit Lakes for $50,000, which is now worth approximately $350,000. Other items sold included a grand piano, a large satellite dish and equipment, an s-curved roll-top desk in perfect condition, and an antique pendulum clock in perfect condition. Some of these items had sentimental value, and others were worth much more than we received. They did temporarily solve our financial problems, but not without a cost.

My first attempt at a new profession was doing motivational seminars with Jerry Maxwell. This had all the makings of a very successful endeavor. Jerry had a name within the insurance industry for doing seminars, and I was a life member of the Million Dollar Round Table. We decided that the first seminar would be in Omaha, Nebraska because the home office of many insurance companies is in Omaha. Jerry would handle disability insurance, and he had his speech down pat. I would talk about life insurance, but I needed someone good at telemarketing who also knew the insurance business to help promote this endeavor while I worked on my part of the seminar.

Into the picture enters a former insurance agent named Hector, who brought me into Mutual Benefit Life when I entered the life insurance business in 1964. Hector had the potential to be a great life insurance salesperson, and he was fantastic on the telephone, but Hector failed in the life insurance business because he kept trying to take what he thought was the easy way out. He tried illegal schemes to solve money problems and spent all of his time trying to keep out of jail. He stayed out of jail because he had tremendous talent, but he was using it in the wrong way.

Hector had been stealing from his boss. He had been doing things like this for years and was caught several times, but was never prosecuted. He was always able to borrow money to pay back what he had stolen and talk his way out of being prosecuted. This time Hector was prosecuted and put on house arrest. He had just come off house arrest and was on probation. I thought of him as a perfect person to do the telemarketing for the seminars. But before I could ask him, he violated his probation, and the prosecutor wanted to put him in jail. He had gotten drunk, gambled, and wrote a check on an account that was closed. Hector told me that he would love to help me put my seminars together if I could only help him avoid going to jail for violating his probation. I knew better, but I was so desperate and he was so good on the telephone that I agreed to help him. I was put on the stand and sworn in. The prosecutor really wanted to put Hector in jail and asked me why I thought he would change. I told the court that I'd known Hector for twenty-seven years and that I knew him as well as anyone. I told them that I would know if he did anything to violate his probation and would immediately turn him in. I also told the court how good he was at telemarketing and that he could be a tremendous help to me and that he could make some very good money by being involved in our seminars. The judge knew Lynda and I and was concerned that Hector might hurt us financially. I made a joke and said, "We are so broke that there isn't any way to hurt us." Boy was I wrong.

Hector had to get permission from his probation officer to go to Omaha with me for the day to find a place to hold our seminar and to check with the sales managers of several insurance companies to see what they thought about our idea. While we were in Omaha, we picked up a phonebook so that Hector could make his calls. Before we went to Omaha, Hector said he didn't have any decent clothes and wondered if I could advance him some money to buy a suit. Mistake number one. I charged the suit, shirt, tie, shoes, and even socks. Hector went all the way. Hector was a very good-looking man, about six-three with curly hair, who made a great impression on everyone he met. We went to Omaha and rented a nice hall for the seminar. I had to make a $100 deposit to hold the hall. We went back to Fargo and had tickets printed with the date, the price, the name of the hall, and our names. We also made up some brochures. Of course, all of this cost more money.

We had given ourselves about six weeks to sell the tickets and get ready for the seminar. Every day Hector would come to my house, go into my office, and start making phone calls. Or so I thought. Hector took a lot of smoke breaks but appeared to be putting in quite a few hours phoning. Almost every day Hector would ask me for $10 to $15 for cigarettes, food, etc. Hector diligently kept track of all the advances. We were trying to sell at least three hundred tickets so that each one of us, including Hector, could make about $5,000 less expenses. After several weeks, Hector started leaving earlier in the day, so he wasn't putting in as much time phoning. At this time, Hector said he had about two hundred tickets sold and had approximately another one hundred and fifty pending. When I asked him why the checks weren't coming in, he said he was dealing with the sales managers of the insurance companies and that they were going to pay for their agents and were waiting to get a final tally before they sent the money. One day, after almost a month, Hector didn't show up for work. He had told his probation officer that he sold all the tickets needed for the seminar and that he wanted to go to Minneapolis for several weeks to sell pressure washers for a fellow he had been in partnership with in the past.

I started calling the names that Hector said had bought twenty tickets here and thirty tickets there. When I got done with my phoning, Hector had actually sold only five tickets. He had called sales managers and told them to sell the tickets which, of course, they did not do. I spent a week on the telephone and sold thirty tickets to make the total thirty-five. Jerry and I were still going to do the seminar just for practice. A general agent who had bought some tickets told me to postpone the seminar until the next fall. He was president of the Health Underwriters Association in Omaha. He said that each fall they did a fundraiser, and they could sell at least five hundred tickets for our seminar. They would take $20 from each ticket, and Jerry and I could take $30. That was $15,000 for Jerry and me to split, but by the next fall, they decided not to do it.

With the clothes, advances, Omaha trip, brochures, hall deposit, advertising in Omaha papers, and long-distance phone bill, good old Hector had nailed me for a few thousand dollars. My very poor judgment and Hector's hidden handicaps and brilliant misuse of talents put me further in the hole. Hector's hidden handicaps demonstrate how someone can destroy his life and waste so much talent. Hector got divorced, hurt his children badly, and borrowed enough money from his dad, mother, brother, and several friends to hurt them financially for the rest of their lives. My experience with Hector made me realize how difficult the road to recovery would be from the hidden handicaps caused by rebating. This recovery would be a nightmare compared to the relative ease in which I overcame my physical disability. Financially and emotionally, the rebating is still affecting me.

Within several weeks after I surrendered my insurance licenses, I started going to counseling. I met Reverend Brunsberg through a mutual friend. Reverend Brunsberg ran a non-profit organization called "The Lost and Found Ministry." He and his staff work with all types of addictions, specializing in substance abuse. I went to counseling with Reverend Brunsberg almost every week until June of 2000, when he had to retire because of health problems. He helped me greatly in fighting the depression that came from the rebating. Most importantly, he helped me identify and eliminate many hidden handicaps, including my gambling problem. A normal session would involve talking about problems I'd had within the last week, sometimes emotional, sometimes business. We talked about everything. Sometimes he would tell me about his problems as examples of how to handle my own. Reverend Brunsberg became a lot more than a counselor; he became a very dear friend. Without Reverend Brunsberg's help, I would probably be in a nursing home today.

This rebating incident and the resulting loss of my insurance license made me realize that I was not invincible and that there were consequences to my actions. As I pointed out earlier, with all the successful stealing and cheating I had done in college, I came to believe that I was invincible. You would think that I would learn after my accident that I wasn't invincible, but I didn't. Somehow I just interpreted that to be an "accident," not a result of continuing to drive when I was tired. Also, since I was able to make good money after the accident selling insurance, I was able to maintain the belief that I was invincible. After I lost my insurance licenses and the business attempts failed, I could no longer maintain that fantasy. I had known before I got caught rebating that I could lose my license, but I didn't really believe I would lose my license, and I hadn't thought about what the consequences of that happening would be. However, because of the rebating, I learned that actions have consequences and that these consequences can be severe. I am not invincible; in fact, I am barely able to support myself and continually face the very real possibility of having to move into a nursing home. Since I could no longer deny or resist this fact, I had to work on correcting this hidden handicap through counseling, which I have done.

Although the realization that I was not invincible brought me to counseling, once I was there, I finally decided it was time to face my hidden handicaps, including my problem with anger that I mentioned earlier. I went to counseling once a week for ten years. I had gone to counseling earlier in my marriage, but never stuck with it long enough for it to do much good. Thank God I must have had some redeeming qualities because my wife stayed with me a long time, and I'm still on good terms with the rest of my family. While telling me about my shortcomings, my ex-wife did say that I was the most generous person she'd ever known, and one of the smartest. I've also always had a lot of friends and acquaintances. I've treated them better than I've treated my family, and so my anger didn't drive them away. I was getting rid of most of my anger on the people I love the most. Why do so many of us do this? I am still working on getting better, but there are probably a few bumps down the road. I never would have made the progress that I have made without counseling. Once I started going to counseling consistently, my anger started to lessen. And since dealing with my gambling problem, the changes have been even more rapid. I feel a lot happier now, and I think contentment is just around the corner.

In order to solve hidden handicaps, you need to change your thinking, habits, and lifestyle. To do this, a doctor or counselor is often needed. There is a way to lessen the effects of your hidden handicaps while you are in the working stage of getting rid of them.

For some people, this method may work to eliminate a hidden handicap. It can also be used just to have a more positive attitude everyday. This concept is used by Life's Missing Link, a non-profit organization started by Jim Marshall, former captain of the Minnesota Vikings for seventeen years. According to their philosophy (which I completely subscribe to), reality is created from the inside out, not from the outside in. Your thought process creates reality from moment to moment, all day long. When you act on them, you create your reality.

To explain how this can be, I want to talk about two different insurance salespeople. The first life insurance salesperson wakes up in the morning, and it is raining hard. Many thoughts flash through his mind. However, only the thoughts he acts on become reality. Let's say one of the thoughts that passes through his mind and he acts on is: "It's going to be a horrible day for selling. People won't want to see salespeople or buy anything. Some will have water leaking in their basements, and they'll have to take care of that. Others will have trouble with their cars and will be busy getting them fixed. I'm just going to go to the office and do some paper work. I'm not going to try to sell anything." The second insurance salesperson wakes up, and it is also raining hard. All kinds of thoughts go through her head also. But she takes action on a different thought: "What a great day for selling. People will be staying in their offices or homes because it is raining so hard. No one will be playing tennis or golf or working in their yards. I'm going to go to the office and make a bunch of phone calls for appointments. I may even get an appointment or two today. I'll brighten somebody's day by taking him or her out for lunch and maybe have another interview for supper. I'll brighten people's spirits by saying things like: the farmers needed the rain or our lawns were getting pretty brown or anything else that will pep them up. I'm going to have a great day today." The same rain brought two completely different realities. So you see, a person's thought process controls their reality.

Realizing that your thought process controls your reality can help you overcome your hidden handicaps. For example, let's say you are a person who has anger as a hidden handicap. You go to pick up your car that was just fixed, and the bill is twice as much as you thought it would be. Sound like a familiar story? A wide range of thoughts start running through your mind: you could kill the mechanic, break every bone in his body, hit him once in the stomach, scream and yell, threaten to take him to the Better Business Bureau, tear up the bill and not pay him, or just pay the bill and not say anything, as it won't do you any good. All the options have consequences ranging from the electric chair, charges of assault and battery, one more place in town that you can't take your car to get fixed, or your blood pressure going up and feeling stressed all for nothing. You can use common sense to process each thought and figure out which consequence you would want. Since you are an angry person, screaming and yelling is most likely your normal response. But common sense tells you that you'll have to pay the bill anyway and that there are already six garages in town that will not fix your car. So after thinking it over, you pay the bill and leave. Your thought process created a peaceful reality. Think of all the other disastrous realities you could have created. So now you see that reality does not cause your thought process. The thought process causes your reality. It is true that the bill was high, but what you did about it caused your reality. So if you can learn to take a little time in making decisions and also use common sense, you can start to overcome your hidden handicaps, keep them in check while you're working on them, and avoid a lot of bad experiences.

Controlling your thought process is different than using willpower. You can't solve hidden handicaps with just willpower. You've heard the expression that someone is on a "dry drunk." As you know, that means they aren't drinking. They are using willpower alone to stay away from alcohol, but the thinking and problems that caused them to drink were never resolved. They haven't changed their thought process, and they're not using common sense. They've simply stopped drinking alcohol, but they still have many unknown hidden handicaps that continue to affect their lives. These hidden handicaps differ from alcoholism, but they are still demons to the alcoholic and inflict damage on the alcoholic and the alcoholic's family and friends. I have seen people stop addictions that were hidden from most people with willpower only, but they never took care of the problems that were causing their addictions. In most cases, new addictions such as a bad temper took the place of the old addiction, and family and friends almost wished they would go back to their old addiction. Willpower alone just doesn't work because it doesn't address the hidden handicap that's causing the problem.

Everyone should do some soul searching to discover hidden handicaps that are negatively affecting them and causing problems in their everyday living. The important thing is to search deep so that you don't stop at the first problem that you find. This problem could just be a symptom of a deeper problem that you had been repressing for a long time. For example, you have, oh let's say, a bad temper that is causing you problems with your family, friends, and your work relationships. You try to solve your problems by not getting angry anymore. You are doing this with willpower. After so long, that doesn't work anymore, and your temper may be worse than it was before. If you had dug deeper, you would have remembered that your dad had a terrible temper and that he took it out on you from the time you were a small child. You built up a lot of resentment for your dad, and now you're taking it out on other people. If you do look deep and discover and correct your hidden handicaps, you'll be happier than you can imagine, and you'll look back and see that you were more unhappy than you realized. You had more demons than you thought you had and hurt more people than you realized. Looking at hidden handicaps is a painful process but well worth it for you and all your loved ones.

Demons, devils, or whatever you want to call them are unbelievably powerful. Once they get inside your head, they can destroy you. Most of the time, the only way to stop them is to find the door that they're coming in and lock it. Finding that door can be extremely hard, and some of us never find it. Sometimes we find it and close it enough that we stop most of the demons from coming in, but a few small ones still squeeze their way through. Some people can have small demons that affect their lives to a smaller degree. They're affected at times but can carry on pretty normal lives. Others have demons that are a little larger and probably make their families dysfunctional, but they still live fairly normal lives. People who are not close to them don't see their struggles. Then we have the people with the monster demons. Everyone can usually see those people suffering. Most people view these people as immoral, stupid, or selfish, or all of the above.

Each person has different personal demons for the same addiction or hidden handicap. In other words, if two people have a gambling problem, more than likely their addiction is not caused by the same reason. This is what makes it so hard to get people to change their thought processes in order to get rid of their addictions or problems. If you break your leg, every orthopedic surgeon would probably treat you pretty much the same, no matter what caused it. But if you have a drug addiction or gambling addiction or depression, you need to treat the source of the problem. Because the source is different for almost everyone, counselors and psychologists find it hard to detect the source of the problem. Too many times people get treated for their symptoms, and the real core of the problem is never discovered. Through motivation and willpower, those people can seem to be in recovery. But after a period of time, they go back to their addiction because the real cause was never discovered and treated. Another problem can be that the counselor may find what appears to be the real problem, so that's what they treat. Both the addict and the counselor think they're on the right track, and they appear to be well on the road to recovery. Maybe after a year, the addiction or problem resurfaces, and the person with the problem and his/her counselor do some more digging and find out that the hidden handicap that they thought was the problem was also caused by another problem that had been repressed from childhood. The person needs to solve that problem before their complete thought process could be changed and they could go on to a successful recovery.

An example is a man we'll call Roger, who had a wife and children and a severe drinking problem. I, for one, thought Roger's problem was a dysfunctional family life when he was a kid. Roger quit drinking two or three times because he loved his children, but his recovery never lasted very long. Roger finally went to a special treatment program, which specialized in deep-seated problems. It turns out that Roger was sexually molested many times by a family friend. This happened when he was very young, and he was afraid to tell anyone about it. He repressed it so well that it didn't really come out until he went to that special treatment center. By the time they found the real hidden handicap, the damage had been done to his family life. Roger and his wife got a divorce, and he lives far away from his family. The last I heard he was in a halfway house doing pretty well but was afraid to go back out on his own. Although it may not seem like it at the time, the pain and damage that come from not addressing a hidden handicap are often worse than the pain of facing and fixing the hidden handicap.

The best way to deal with a hidden handicap is to talk to someone about the problem and to start doing something about it immediately. Your hidden handicap is at its worst as long as it is a secret, so ninety-nine percent of the time you are better off getting help from a counselor, clergy member, doctor, psychologist, psychiatrist, financial planner, or a support group that fits your needs instead of trying to go it alone. Sometimes we're in line for an emotional overhaul and need all of the above. Feeling good is obviously the best way to live, both for ourselves and for all the people around us. But for some reason, a lot of us keep making it tough on ourselves by continuing to do things that make us miserable. I think we do this for at least a couple of reasons. One reason is that we use these hidden handicaps as excuses for lack of accomplishments in our lives; however, using them as excuses is really taking the hard way out. The second reason we keep doing something that makes us miserable is that someplace in our destructive actions or medical problems, we find short periods of highs where we get endorphins working, like I did with gambling. I have been able to replace the highs of gambling by spending more time with my sons and daughters, grandchildren, and friends. And I certainly don't miss the lows. I still have to scramble for money, but now it is not for a gambling loss, so I don't feel the need to lie to my friends. It's amazing that we will torture ourselves with the demons of a hidden handicap for the small amount of pleasure that it gives us. That seems to be the nature of the beast, and that is why we must talk to friends or counselors to put things into perspective. It generally takes hard work to make us feel better. But we need to change our way of thinking in order to realize that hard work and trying our best is accomplishment enough in our lives. I still think about gambling, but when the thought enters my mind I don't take action on it. I'm sure many of you still think about doing things that you know will cause you a problem, but you need to use common sense and not take action on these thoughts. When we realize this, we will be taking the easy way out, and success will follow.

One of the barriers to changing our way of thinking and overcoming a hidden handicap is guilt. As you know, guilt is associated with most problems. Unfortunately, we are often hesitant to forgive ourselves, even if we are religious and know that God forgives us. Still, forgiving ourselves is a must. Nothing else will work until we stop blaming ourselves for whatever problem or obstacle we need to overcome. Everyone deserves to be happy. Learn all you can about your problem and get an understanding of why you are better off without this obstacle. Remember, doing something because others want you to do it seldom works in the long run. It may work for awhile, but in order to make it long lasting, you need to understand and believe why it is right for you. After you have overcome your obstacle, all of your business and family relationships will fall into place. And finally, fire all your guns and cannons. Use everything at your disposal to overcome your obstacle. When you put everything together and turn your disability into an ability, then you'll be taking the "easy way out."

I have done this in many ways with my physical disability. When I was a general agent before my accident, I told my agents that the telephone was for making appointments and that major sales were made in person. I was so bullheaded about this I don't know if I would have ever changed my view if I hadn't been in the accident. After I was injured, I obviously had to use the telephone. I developed ways of selling on the phone that I think are better than some of the ways of selling in person. I would make an appointment for a specific time and day and send the prospect all the information that we were going to discuss. Sometimes the printouts might have been fifteen or twenty pages. I numbered all the pages so that it was easy to lead the prospect to the page I wanted to talk about. One of the advantages of the telephone interview is that the prospect usually didn't take other phone calls or talk to his secretary during the interview, as would frequently happen with an in-person interview. Other advantages are obvious. I could have many more appointments in a day, it was less expensive, and if someone stood me up for an appointment, I was only seconds away from my next interview. I would also send the client all the applications and would close just like a personal interview. He would fill out the application, sign it, write out a check, and send it back. In this way, I was able to do much more business in a day than I could before my accident.

Another way I turned my physical disability into an advantage is by talking to a client or prospective client about the service they would now receive from me. I would tell them that before my accident I had many hobbies, went on many business trips, and had a young family. It was very difficult to find me when they had a service problem or a question. Today they can almost always find me twenty-four hours a day. My main recreation is working. I have received many favorable comments on the service I provide. Clients like to be able to call at odd hours with their questions.

In my life, I've been lucky to have reached many high peaks and have had the misfortune to reach many low valleys. The peaks have far outweighed the valleys. Remembering the joy of the good things in your life helps you when you have a major problem. You also need an inner strength and an understanding of yourself to overcome the problems of hidden handicaps that you face in your life. That's why you need to talk to someone about your hidden handicaps immediately. You can start by talking to a friend, but then you should talk to a counselor, psychologist, psychiatrist, member of the clergy, doctor, financial planner, or support group. There are many support groups, and it's easy to find the one that fits your needs. If you end up in a support group, you will probably be helping yourself and helping others at the same time. I have raised thousands of dollars for the Spinal Cord Society for research. I wish I could raise money every day because I feel so good at the end of the day. I can't do it because I need to make money to pay my bills and stay at home. Being involved in a self-help group is an example of "taking the easy way out."

My goal in writing this book is to help other people and to try to give back an ounce of the help they have given me. If you want to get something out of this book, you need to take action right now. I have read many books with a message, and I have listened to hundreds of motivating seminars. Some of them you walk away from with nothing. But most of them have at least one idea that, if you did something about it, would improve your quality of life. I have gone away from reading some of these books or attending some of these seminars with the best of intentions, and most of the time, in a few days, the message has been lost. I don't want this to happen to you after reading my book. I insist that you get at least one thing out of this book that will make you feel better. I know that everyone reading this book has at least one hidden handicap and that more than likely, something you have read has revealed one of your hidden handicaps. There isn't anyone whose life is so perfect that they don't need to make a change. Some people are pretty happy, and the change might be subtle. With others, the changes might be mind-boggling. So when you've finished this chapter, close up the book and go find a person who you feel you can talk to about your inner self. Don't try to do this. Do it! If you say you're going to do something tomorrow, you're procrastinating and not taking action (which as I noted two chapters ago is another hidden handicap). Take one thing out of this chapter and start making a change in your life today. Tell the person about something you've never told anyone and see how much better you feel. Now the process has begun, don't let it die! You deserve to feel good. Make the necessary effort to do so. There isn't a problem in the world that doesn't get smaller when you share it with other people, and there isn't a problem in the world that doesn't get bigger when you keep it a secret. Take action!!! If you are not willing to do this, throw this book in the trash because it will not fulfill its purpose.

Chapter 8

WHEELCHAIR SHOCK

For all you able-bodied people, remember one very important thing: I am permanently disabled, and you are "temporarily abled." Don't get me wrong; I don't want any of you to become disabled. Those of us who have disabilities need all the help we can get. I've lived in my wheelchair because I have had no choice; it's not a lifestyle that a person chooses. However, most people become disabled sometime in their lifetime. The big question is when. If you start with a group of one hundred people, by the time each one of them turns sixty-five, nineteen will have died, sixty-six will be dependent on someone else, and only fifteen will have an income of at least $30,000 and will be financially and physically independent. It is true that becoming disabled happens to most people in their later years; however, it is always tough to deal with. The more knowledge and understanding you have, the better equipped you'll be to deal with people with disabilities and elderly people, whether they are family members, friends, or strangers. You will also be better equipped to handle it if it happens to you.

Many able-bodied people are afraid or uncomfortable around people with physical disabilities, developmental disabilities, illness, or elderly people. Most of these able-bodied people are in the resistance stage of a hidden handicap: they know they have a problem, but they don't want to do anything about it. A few of these able-bodied people are in the denial stage of a hidden handicap; they know they have a problem, but they're in denial about how it's affecting their life. When a friend gets sick or has an accident, these people are unable to go to the hospital to visit them. When the person goes home from the hospital, they still avoid them because they don't know what to say. This is not only hard on the able-bodied person who would like to see their friend, but it's also hard on the person with the disability or sickness who needs their friends to visit them. Overcoming this hidden handicap through awareness can help solve these problems.

One way to become more aware is to become more involved. Remember Charlie, the fellow with Muscular Dystrophy whom I talked about in the chapter "Take the Easy Way Out"? He only had movement of his head and right thumb, and he ran a cigarette and candy stand at St. John's Hospital in Fargo. I had the privilege of helping Charlie for quite a few years. This gave me a lot of preparation for being able to deal with my disability when it was suddenly thrust upon me. Unfortunately, becoming a person with a disability is not like becoming a pharmacist or an engineer; you don't get four or five years of training. It happens, and you immediately have to start dealing with the sickness and/or disability. However, being more involved with those who have a disability or illness can help you prepare a bit.

I didn't get involved with Charlie because I was planning ahead; I got involved because I cared. I was happy to help Charlie whenever I could. Because of some new government regulations, Charlie was forced to move from St. John's Hospital to Villa Maria nursing home. Charlie called me up and asked me if I could come over and help him move, which of course I did. After we got all of his personal belongings put into the pickup, Charlie said there was one more thing we had to do. I wheeled Charlie all over St. John's Hospital, but mostly through the basement. He had approximately $3,000 hidden in fifteen or sixteen places that had been put there by fifteen or sixteen different people. He didn't trust anyone with the whole amount, so each person only knew about his or her spot, and Charlie knew who that person was. It was unbelievable to me that he could remember the names of the people and all the places the money was hidden. From that time on, I kept Charlie's money for him in a checking account in my name. Charlie didn't make as much money at Villa Maria, so when he ran out of money, I would put some in his account so that he could buy the things he needed, including gas and repairs on his van. Every few years, I would buy Charlie a new van. By doing so much with Charlie, I thought I knew everything there was to know about being in a wheelchair. Boy, was I in for a shock. However, I knew a lot more and was more prepared than if I hadn't been involved with Charlie.

Clare Poseley was another person with disabilities who I helped out and took places for about ten or eleven years. Clare had cerebral palsy, but he was able to walk and work. He was the equipment manager for the NDSU Bison, and he just loved it. He lived with his mother, and when she died, he started drinking heavily. Some relatives took him to Jamestown, North Dakota for treatment. While there, they apparently didn't have him walking and doing exercises every day. He came out of there a recovering alcoholic, but his legs, arms, and fingers were so twisted that he couldn't use them anymore. He was put into a nursing home and went from being self-sufficient to being severely disabled in several months. I was angrier about this situation than Clare. He was a very gentle and patient person. Clare was a graduate of NDSU and loved Bison sports. I took him to almost every Bison basketball and football game. We also had him over to the house for many holidays, as he had no family and just a few friends. It was good for my children to associate with Charlie and Clare. My wife Lynda was an RN and was very comfortable with people with disabilities and made them feel very comfortable. Spending time with Clare also helped me get ready for the life I was going to lead.

One of the reasons people hesitate to interact with people with disabilities is because they don't know how to interact with them. When engaging with people with disabilities, here are a few ideas on how to interact with them. First, make them feel comfortable, and second, be more comfortable yourself. If the person is a relative or friend, treat them the same way you treated them before their accident or sickness. If your relationship was one of sarcasm, then don't change it. Don't shy away from their problem, but also don't dwell on it. Do a lot of listening to see how they are handling their problem. When you talk about their disability or sickness, you shouldn't make it worse than it is, but you also shouldn't make it better. To get through tragedies, people need humor. If people can make fun of themselves, they will learn how to deal with their disabilities much sooner. How much humor you use depends on how well you know the person and how they seem to be handling their disability. If for some reason you are thrown into a conversation with a stranger who has a disability, treat them the same way you would treat a stranger who doesn't have a disability.

A lot of people don't know how to talk to someone with disabilities, so they avoid the situation. Although they would rather talk to the person, they don't know what to say. They are right to be cautious, but not to be silent. The most damaging things you can say to someone who has just had a sickness or injury that left them with a disability are, "Things could be worse," or "Things aren't too bad," or "You're not in as bad of shape as Fred." No matter how bad someone's disability is, it can always be worse, but telling them that doesn't help at all. People can only relate to their own situation. If someone who lost their left leg could be Tom Day for a couple of weeks, maybe they'd think their loss wasn't that bad. However, their loss may have been harder for them to adjust to than my disability was for me. Instead of minimizing the loss, the best thing to do is state the facts and talk about things they can and can't do. Acknowledge that they had a bad break and offer encouragement. Just don't use the words "and it could be worse" or "you're not as bad as Fred." Acknowledge that they have a tough road ahead of them, but that you're confident that they can do it. If they're really depressed, do more listening than talking, then wait for a better day to give them a pep talk.

The same ideas apply for talking to someone who has had a disability for awhile. Many times the words we use can be negative and adversely affect people's self-esteem. However, we don't have to use negative words; we can use more neutral terms. For example, don't use the word "afflicted;" use the words "affected by." "Crippled" paints a very negative mental picture; "disabled" is much better. Similarly, "condition" is much better than "disease," and "added responsibility" is much better than "burden." Don't use the word "poor" for someone's health or the words "unfortunate" or "victim."

Instead, describe their condition such as, "Sally has diabetes." Rather than saying "wheelchair bound" or "confined to a wheelchair," say "wheelchair user" or "Sue uses a wheelchair." "Retarded" is a real no-no. Use "mental disability" or "developmental disability." Don't say, "he's crazy," say "he has a mental illness." And don't classify people as "the disabled" or "the deaf." Say "people with disabilities, deafness, or hearing impairments." I make many mistakes regarding words, but by being aware that certain words make people feel good and other words make them feel bad, I make fewer mistakes. If people know which words to avoid and which to use, they should be more comfortable talking to people with disabilities.

Another thing to be aware of when interacting with people with disabilities is that they can talk and think. A rather large segment of the population thinks that people in wheelchairs cannot talk or think. It's amazing to watch them go into "wheelchair shock." When I went to a party with my wife, someone would come up to the two of us and ask her, "What does he eat?" or "What can he drink?" I don't think a lot of people realize what they're doing; I think it's just the way they've been educated by society. For example, the other day I was having lunch in a restaurant. The waitress was very nice and seemed extremely comfortable with me, which is not always the case. She took my order, and we kidded around. She treated me like you should treat a person with a disability—normally. She brought my steak, set it down, and was standing right between me and my attendant. Then she turned to Annette and said, "What kind of steak sauce does he use?" These are the ones who are tough to figure. Most of the time if a waitress or waiter has this type of mentality, they start out asking my attendant what I want. Even though this way of thinking is unintentional, it is very prevalent.

One of my most unbelievable experiences with this type of thinking was when I was getting out of the hospital. I'd been in there about eight months, and my wife said that before I could come home, we needed to hire two nurses to take care of me during the day. I was so anxious to go home that I would have hired the devil himself. I nearly did. Lynda brought two applicants to the hospital, an RN and an LPN, and I hired them. They were to spend six or seven hours at the hospital learning how to take care of me. Everyone, including the nurses from the hospital, lost sight of the fact that I was the only person who spent twenty-four hours a day, seven days a week with Tom Day and who knew all the procedures involving his care. When they first started explaining to my prospective nurses how to do certain things, they completely ignored the fact that I was there. I thought it was a little strange, but it became unbelievable when they put me in the wheelchair and wanted these girls to take me to physical therapy. One of the girls looked right past me and said, "How do we get there?" I knew that my nurse from the hospital would say, "Tom knows how to get there, he's been going there for the past eight months." But low and behold, she started to explain how to get there. I thought that any minute it would dawn on them that I knew the way, so I didn't say anything because I wanted to see how long this would go on. Well, this happened about twenty-four years ago, and I'd probably still be sitting there because I don't think my two nurses would've figured out how to get there. So I finally said, "I think I know the way." And the hospital nurse said, "Well sure, Tom can tell you how to get there." But none of them realized how ridiculous their ten-minute conversation had been. Wheelchair shock is that ingrained in our society.

I had to fire the RN within the first two months because she was unable to see me as anything other than a wheelchair patient. She was a lady in her fifties who tried to run our house like a hospital. For two months, we told her that we didn't want her to wear her nurse's uniform because we didn't want our home to look like a hospital. But every day that she worked, she was dressed in white from her shoes to her hat. She also tried to establish a routine: breakfast at a certain time, exercises, and baths, all on her schedule. I had put up with that for eight months in the hospital and wasn't going to do that anymore. Finally, we told her that we would have to let her go if she showed up in her uniform the next day. Well, the next day she wore it, so we had to let her go. She just wasn't able to conceive of me as anything other than a sick, disabled person.

It's not just individuals who don't know how to treat people with disabilities as people. Businesses are also lacking in this area, even though they shouldn't be. On July 26th, 1990, Congress passed the Americans With Disabilities Act, which went into effect in 1992. The ADA, as it is called, requires that public and private buildings be more accessible for people with disabilities, that public transportation be made available to people with wheelchairs, etc., and that employers hire people with disabilities. Unfortunately, the ADA does not have a lot of teeth, and the government hasn't done a very good job of enforcing the regulations that it passed. For example, almost every business has handicapped parking, but they don't have proper access for people with disabilities and the elderly in their entrances. Also, the employees are not trained how to communicate with people with disabilities, senior citizens, and their family and friends, so frequently employees are inadvertently rude. As a result, people with disabilities, senior citizens, and their attendants do not come back to the business, and sometimes many other family members and friends will not patronize the establishment. However, business owners don't seem to realize that poor treatment of people with disabilities is bad for business. They should because there are fifty-four million people with disabilities in the United States. On average, each one of them has at least two people who care about them; that is more than half of the United States population. Because of the above figures, it is very important for all able-bodied people who are owners or managers of retail establishments to understand and know how to communicate with people with disabilities. If they don't, they will lose a lot of business.

Business owners also don't realize that in failing to make their buildings handicapped accessible, they are also losing many of their elderly clientele. There was a restaurant in Moorhead where I and five or six other friends went for lunch almost every week. They installed a microbrewery and also remodeled the back of the restaurant. The backdoor was a hard door for someone in a wheelchair to get through, so I assumed that they would put in a handicapped accessible door since the handicapped parking was in the back. Instead, they put in a heavier door, not handicapped accessible, making it much harder for a handicapped person to get in. After seeing this, I stopped going to their restaurant, and so did my friends. Recently, this restaurant went out of business. I don't think they failed just because of the way they treated people with disabilities and senior citizens, but I believe their lack of sensitivity carried over into other areas and contributed to their downfall. What many people don't understand is that senior citizens use handicapped accessible doors as much as people in wheelchairs. I see senior citizens using these doors all the time. Regular doors are just too heavy for them to open. If they can't get in, the company loses their business.

In addition to having inadequate access to their buildings, many businesses also lose money because they don't know how to treat their customers who have disabilities. My son, Mike, sells cars at Harold's Chevrolet in Minneapolis. Recently, Mike talked to a young man in a wheelchair who was paralyzed from the waist down. He saw the young man in the wheelchair and his friend leaving the new car lot and went over to visit with them. The man in the wheelchair told Mike he was leaving because one of Mike's co-workers had done all his talking to his friend and not to him. He told Mike that he was looking for a corvette, but at almost every dealership he had visited, the salespeople talked mainly to his friend and sometimes didn't talk to him at all. This is probably the number one problem faced by people with disabilities. The salesperson usually talks to the family member or caregiver attending to the person with the disability instead of the person with the disability. People with disabilities are usually fighting low self-esteem and need to be treated with respect. It is also just common sense to talk to the person who is doing the buying. Many times salespeople assume that a person in a wheelchair doesn't have any money. That is not necessarily the case. This young man had been looking for a car for more than a year but had not purchased one partly because he had not found the one he wanted, but mainly because of the way the salespeople had treated him. In either case, it wasn't because he didn't have the money. The young man in the wheelchair purchased a corvette from my son, Mike, and wrote out a check that day for more than $48,000.

When companies fail to see people with disabilities as people, they lose business opportunities in sales and in potential employees. In the past, when employers were forced to hire minorities, many times they did not screen or interview the minority person. They simply filled their quotas or hired their token minority. Employers should interview and screen people with disabilities the same as they would anyone else. If a person was lazy before he or she had the disability, he or she will be lazy after they have the disability. Whatever weaknesses they had before will be greater, but whatever strengths they had will be greater as well. Also, when people get a disability, they are usually unable to participate in the same leisure activities as before. Take me for example. Before I was hurt, I did things with my family and played golf every day from April to September. I played tennis once or twice a week. I swam, water-skied, bowled, played softball, basketball, touch football, and from time to time went to bars. In between those activities, I even found some time to work. I am no longer able to do most of those activities, so my interest is in my work and my family. I work ten to twelve hours a day. If someone hired me, they'd be getting the best employee, abled or disabled, they could find. So if you find the right people with disabilities, they will make great employees.

Perhaps some of the least handicapped accessible buildings are in the sports industry. I go to a lot of sporting events, some plays, movies, operas, etc. The handicapped seating at all the events, except athletics, is usually good. The athletic events that I attend regularly have the worst seating. In Fargo, I get treated very well at all the high schools and colleges. The only problem is that I couldn't get a real good seat if I paid $1,000. I'd still be in the end zone for football games and behind the basket at basketball games. I've had the most problems at sporting events in the Fargodome. The building was built with $50 million of taxpayer's money, and they've put millions of dollars in it since. When completed, it had no handicapped seating for sporting events. People with disabilities are put in aisles in all four corners. People walk in front of, over, and behind you.

The worst problem for people with disabilities is the mentality of the people who run these events. They have this archaic rule that a person in a wheelchair can only have one person (an attendant) with them. If you wanted to take a group of six to a sporting event and the ticket sellers told you that only two of you could go together, you wouldn't put up with it. Why is someone in a wheelchair different? Since I am paralyzed from the neck down, my attendants accompany me to events to take care of my personal and medical needs. I have to buy two tickets to a game, pay for two meals, and pay someone $7 to $10 an hour to be at the game with me. I don't mind this because it's the baggage that comes with the wheelchair. But I should be able to take family and friends to events and sit with them. I love to go to athletic events at North Dakota State University, my alma mater. At women's volleyball and men's wrestling, the seats are great. Women and men's basketball and football is a different story. For seven years, I worked to get equal treatment for people with disabilities. I would spend most of the time at a football or basketball event struggling to get a view of the game. There were usually people standing in front of me.

A year ago, I won a small victory. In football, even though I'm in the end zone, I'm in an area where people no longer block my view because they roped off the row of seats in front of me. It's also roped off at either end, so it no longer can be used as an aisle. I can bring my attendant and still have family and friends come as well. For other people in wheelchairs, they bought two platforms. One is in the end zone and can hold ten to twelve people. The other one was promised by the athletic director to be put on the thirty-yard line. However, in eight or nine years, we've never seen it up. We have a new athletic director now, so maybe things will change. At basketball games, the situation has also improved for people in wheelchairs. We don't have people standing in front of us, and we can take more than one person with us to a game. It's been a fun two years. I have fought hard for my rights, but people with disabilities shouldn't have to fight to be able to go to a game with their family or friends.

Although it has been a battle to go to some sporting events and see the game, there have been more positive experiences than negative. I went to almost every single out-of-town event that my boys and girls participated in. I remember driving seven hundred miles one way to watch my son, Joe, play football at University of Nebraska at Kearny. After driving all that way, we almost didn't get to park in the end zone to see the game. We ran into a very mean-spirited person. One person can temporarily make you forget all the nice people who help you. For those of you with whom I've had battles, I hope you learn to treat people with disabilities with more dignity and sensitivity. You may end up with a disability yourself, and it will be a tough way for you to learn how important that is. I suggest that you learn while you're still in good shape. To those of you who have helped me on two or three trips to your school for athletic events, I thank you. For the people of Grand Forks and especially the University of North Dakota, you have treated me the best of any place out of town. Finally, to those of you in the Fargo-Moorhead area who continuously help me to get the best seat possible at sporting events or a good place to park my van to watch football games, I thank you profusely. I imagine that for the most part all of you who have helped me know who you are. You are great human beings.

Although I've been trying to make you more aware of how to treat people with disabilities, there is another group of people who needs to be acknowledged too. The forgotten people when someone gets sick or injured are the caregivers. I know in my case everyone would ask, "How is Tom?" Almost no one thought about my wife and children. I had suffered many losses, but so had they. The person with the disability cannot escape from their losses; it's just a matter of how they handle them. But all the people who take care of them have choices. First of all, my family didn't have to bring me home, and as severe as my disability is, I don't think anyone would have blamed them. If it weren't for my wife, children, friends, relatives, and all the hundreds of caregivers who have worked for me the last twenty-four years, I wouldn't be writing this book. I would have been in a nursing home long ago, and the quality of my life would have been nothing compared to what it has been living in my own home. So when you have a friend or relative who becomes sick or injured and ends up needing help, don't forget the caregivers. Ask them how they're doing and if they need any help.

My family decided to bring me home from the hospital, and they had the major role of taking care of me from the beginning. Even though I've now hired people to provide me with constant care, my family still helps me in other ways. The up side of my family helping me was that they learned a lot about what it's like to have a disability, and they have a sensitivity for people with disabilities, whether the disability is the result of an accident or a sickness. The downside was they had to make a lot of sacrifices to help me. I also was not a very easy person to take care of. I had very little patience and expected perfection. I yelled at all of them when they didn't have it coming. Unfortunately, they came out of the experience with a lot of hidden handicaps that they are still working on. I'm still working to have more patience and make amends for the way I treated them. There is still some pain that needs to be worked out, but we talk about it, and we're coming closer to being a happy family. It has been my observation that whenever a family member is a caregiver, there are issues that come up that they have to deal with. Most of the time, they suppress these feelings because they feel guilty and don't want to hurt the feelings of the person with the disability. These again are hidden handicaps that eventually need to be dealt with.

The purpose of this chapter is to inform all of you who are able-bodied about people with disabilities. This will involve challenging people's stereotypes regarding people with disabilities. People with disabilities have feelings that are as individual and different as any other group. We are living in a world that often overlooks us and presents us with extra difficulties such as limited access to amenities and facilities. My objective is to get people to focus on our abilities and needs as people—to look past the wheelchair or the disability and to see the person individually. My good friends see all the things that I can accomplish and most of the time they forget that I have a disability.

Most of the time people who have a hidden handicap regarding people with disabilities and/or sick people are uncomfortable when forced to be in their presence or go to great lengths to avoid them altogether. As a person gets older, this problem grows. Friends and relatives start having problems with their health. When it hits your parents, it is really hard to avoid. Why not take the easy way out and force yourself to interact with people with disabilities or illnesses now? It will be hard at first, but it will become easier and easier.

People who couldn't visit me at first now don't even think of me as having a disability. Think of how nice it will be to help your parents, friends, and relatives without being uncomfortable. You will get great satisfaction from helping them, and they will know that it doesn't bother you. It's really hard for me to be around someone who is uncomfortable with me. Someday you may be sick or have a disability (let's hope that doesn't happen); if you address this hidden handicap now, not only will you better understand what you may go through, but also you won't be afraid.

•

Chapter 9

BEHIND THE SCENES

This chapter could be titled, "Everything You Didn't Want to Know about People with Disabilities." I took care of two people with disabilities before I got hurt, so I had some idea of what it takes to get people with disabilities up in the morning, what their needs are during the day, and what it takes to put them to bed at night. However, I really didn't know as much as I thought I did. One example is itching. I never dreamed that would be one of my number one enemies. When the girl taking care of me leaves me at home for a half hour I have the phone for emergencies but the phone won't scratch me, sometimes it almost drives me crazy. There are other examples but itching is by far the worst. Able-bodied people don't even realize how much they itch themselves. I think that most able-bodied people have no idea how much work is involved in taking care of a person with disabilities. For many of the people with disabilities I know, including myself, our care creates several hidden handicaps. These hidden handicaps are ones we really can't change. But I'd like to follow my own advice because maybe it will help to talk about it, if only so that able-bodied people will know why sometimes we can't make early morning appointments. (I am so dependent on other people that if one of my attendants doesn't show up, is late, or gets sick during the day, it affects my whole schedule.) More importantly, I'd like to share my experiences to give you my perspective on what it's like to take care of a person with a disability so that when it happens to you or someone you love, you will be better prepared to deal with it. Hopefully, it will also make you more compassionate for the people with disabilities and illness in your life right now.

I have three college girls who live in my home and take care of me from ten at night until eight every morning. They each take ten nights a month. They also work the Monday through Friday evening shifts from five to ten and the weekends. There is one more person who does not live here, but who works part-time to help the other three with the evening shifts and the weekends. Another girl works days from eight to five, Monday through Friday. This is my only full-time employee, and because I do so much during the daytime, this girl has to be smart and have a wide range of talents. With low unemployment, it has become harder to find good employees. However, over the years, I have had some of the most tremendous girls in the world. They learn an awful lot at this job about life and business. Many of them have gone on to very good jobs using my job as a reference.

Every morning, a girl, who has stayed over night in the bedroom across the hall, comes into my room at about seven forty-five. She opens the blinds and then takes off the footboard near the end of my bed that keeps me from sliding down during the night. Then she takes off the foot braces I have on each foot, the leg splints, and the arm splints. All of these are necessary for my arms and legs so that they do not curl into positions where I would be unable to sit in a wheelchair. Next, she changes my night bag to a day bag, which is connected to my catheter. This has to be done with a sterile technique, or I will get more bladder infections than I currently get. The attendant then checks my blood sugar (I am a diabetic) and records the results in our logbook. By then, the girl who works eight to five has arrived, and they do my range-of-motion exercises. These consist of six different exercises on each arm. They then pull me down in bed and do four more range of motion exercises on each leg. Every other day, they irrigate my bladder. They use a syringe to put 30cc of Renacidin into my bladder and let it stay there for ten minutes. This is done to cleanse and extend my bladder. When that is done, they change my pants and pull up my stockings, which go to the top of my thighs. These stockings help with circulation and prevent blood clots. The attendants also have to change the bandage that covers the area where my Foley catheter goes into my bladder. This is cleaned and re-bandaged every other day. Then they wash me up between the legs and pull up my pants.

The attendant/secretary then rolls me over on my side and pulls down my pants. First, she checks my butt for any new pressure sores or checks to see how the one I usually have is doing. Then I do my bowel program. This program can take anywhere from ten minutes to three hours. On days that I am not planning anything except to work in the house, we don't have to worry about how long it takes. But on a morning that I have a nine o'clock appointment, it can be a problem. This is why I have to start at five if I want to make sure that I am going to get to the appointment on time. Because of this, I try and avoid early morning appointments. After my bowel program is completed, the secretary/attendant gives me a bed bath and shaves me. She then puts a Hoyer pad under me. Bars go in either end on both sides and then chains are hooked to the bars on either end. She then hooks a ceiling lift to the chains. This talented person then has to push me to a sitting position, make sure that my arms get pushed forward to avoid the chains, and run the power switch all at the same time. Then she wheels me around the track on the ceiling and has me hovering over the chair. There's a Roho cushion on the wheelchair that has been shaken and put in the chair strategically. She lowers me to a position just above the Roho cushion. The chair is then moved one way or the other so that I am exactly in the center. Then she pushes my knees so that I am to the back of the chair and lets me down. She has to run her hand under my ishiam bone on each cheek and my tailbone to make sure that there is just the right amount of air between me and the bottom of the cushion. Too much air can cause problems, and not enough air is disastrous. I have had three bad pressure sores from the air going out of my cushion. Two of them kept me in bed for six months, and one of them kept me in bed for almost a year with three surgeries. She then puts on my shirt and sweater, and I am ready for the day. This could have taken anywhere from forty-five minutes to four hours. A lot of it depends on how my bowels reacted that day, but some of it depends on the relative talent of the girl getting me up. Some of the good ones are really fast.

With all the business things that I do in a day, I need a very sharp secretary. I have been very lucky to find many extremely gifted secretaries who are also able to do my personal care. Many times we have wished that we had recorded everything ever said in this room. If you didn't see it and just heard it, it would sound pretty wild. I have a lot of problems with pressure sores, and this also affects my day because it sometimes limits the time I can be in my wheelchair. When I have a pressure sore, my friend, Dr. John Sarbacker, comes over to look at it. When he is deciding what to put on it, he usually quotes one of his doctor instructors who said, "You can put cow dung on a pressure sore, and it will heal it if you stay off of it." This is his subtle way of telling me to spend less time in my wheelchair. He knows how I hate to stay in bed. I kid Dr. Sarabacker that he can't recognize me unless he is looking at my butt. If I had a dollar for everyone who has seen my butt, I'd be wealthy. When I first got hurt, all of these personal cares were embarrassing, but after twenty-four years, I've lost my modesty.

During the day, my leg bag has to be emptied three or four times depending on how much water or liquid I drink. I can tell when it is full because I get the chills and I start sweating. Sometimes this happens at very inappropriate times, and we have to be very creative to find a place and a way to empty the bag, as conventional bathrooms do not work for me. We use a bucket, or a pop cup, or whatever, and wherever!

The last description of things that have to be done out of sight involves a funny story. When I get a cold, I don't have the muscles in my chest to cough up the phlegm. So the only way to get it out is for me to take a deep breath and for the girls to push on my stomach at the same time. We continue to do this five to ten times until I get something up. Another way to do it, when that way doesn't work, is for me again to take a deep breath and for them to push my back so that I go forward to my knees to help get the phlegm up. I then take another deep breath, and they push again. They continue this until something comes up. If someone who didn't know what was going on were to see this procedure, they would think my attendants were trying to kill me.

One night, when I had a bad cold, I was addicted to gambling enough to go run a poker tournament that I had scheduled some weeks before. This tournament was being held in a warehouse-type building where there were businesses on either side of a big parking lot. My attendant and I pulled into this parking lot, which was pretty full since there was a restaurant nearby. We had to park closer to the businesses across the parking lot. I had about thirty players inside waiting for the tournament to start. I was late, and they could not start without me. Before I went in, I wanted my attendant to get up some phlegm so that I would be good for about a half an hour before I had to go in the back room and have her push me again. She pushed from the front, and that wasn't working very well, so she went behind the wheelchair and pushed from the back. It took us about fifteen minutes, but finally my lungs were cleared out for awhile.

What we didn't know was when we had parked, there was a fellow standing over in front of a business watching us, and he thought I was either dying or that she was trying to kill me. He called 911 and told them there was an emergency. Just as we were going to get out of the van, we heard sirens blaring and saw vehicles heading for the van—a fire truck, an ambulance, and two police cars. They all pulled up to the front of the van, and we had no idea why they were there. In the meantime, all the poker players heard the sirens, and the thirty of them came out into the parking lot with the door open and poker tables with poker chips in full view. I told the girl with me to run over and tell them to get back in the building and lock the door. In the meantime, all these emergency officials opened the van door and asked me what was wrong. They told me that a man had called in and said it looked like someone in a wheelchair was dying or being abused. I explained to them that I just had a cold and that this was the only way that I could get the phlegm up. I thanked them for their concern and breathed a sigh of relief as they drove away. They had not spotted the poker players with the poker tables inside. There are a lot of other things that people in wheelchairs experience that most able-bodied people don't realize. I thought I would just highlight some of them.

I have said that I am used to living in a wheelchair and that it doesn't really bother me that much anymore. That is true. I have a saying that if I could just be a quadriplegic and not have any other problems I would be happy. I think most people who look at someone in a wheelchair feel that being in a wheelchair and the restrictions it causes are what's really hard. For me, that is not true. In my case, being in the wheelchair, traveling in the wheelchair, and working with the limitations of the wheelchair are not a problem. I have accepted the fact that I am in a wheelchair and that there's nothing I can do about it. It's all the other things that are difficult. For example, I have diabetes. That's an extra I'm not excited about. I also have had pre-cancer of the esophagus. Many days I am warm and not sweating when I'm up in my wheelchair, and then I'm just a quad. I love it! However, on some days, I sweat and get the chills for some unknown reason. Sometimes this won't happen for a year, and sometimes I'll have it for three to four months at a time. If I lay my chair back flat for about five minutes, then sometimes it will go away for half an hour, or three hours, or all day. We have tried everything and cannot understand what is causing this. When I go to bed, it immediately stops. When I get a cold, as explained before, that disrupts my routine quite a bit. It makes it difficult to work or to go to any outdoor events. I just want to be a quad with no other problems.

I am pretty used to all the personal cares described above. But they still make it difficult to get to places early in the morning and sometimes to be on time any time of the day. However, the most difficult part of these cares is the cost. My twenty-four-hour-a-day care plus my medications and medical supplies cost about $6,000 a month. I also have the cost of maintaining a wheelchair van with a lift and the expense associated with getting five miles to the gallon. Probably one of the toughest and most frustrating parts of my situation is the continual battle to have enough people to cover all the shifts twenty-four hours a day. I get a girl I really like and who is trained in so well that she can read my mind, and all of a sudden, she's gone. And I know I can't replace her. Then I'll maybe go through two or three girls who don't work out. And then I'll find another winner. And so it goes. Also the cost of advertising for these girls runs between $700 and $1,000 per year. Some years, I'm lucky and have the same crew for the whole year. These costs and personnel issues are a few more of the hidden handicaps that come with my physical   disabilities.

I've also learned a lesson the hard way about firing my help. One of the first two nurses we hired after I came home from the hospital was an LPN who was a young girl in her twenties. After several weeks, I found out she was quite heavily addicted to drugs. Her drug of choice was speed. Near the end of each month, she and her husband would run out of money. She would then be out of speed for a few days. When she was on speed, she flew around the room and was pleasant, but when she ran out of the drug, she really got mean. One day, she had me flat on the bed in preparation for getting me into the wheelchair. I have an electronic device on the side of my bed that allows me to control most of the things in my room including the telephone. When laid flat, I cannot use this device, and I'm completely helpless. She became very abusive while I was lying there, and I lost my temper and did something really dumb. I fired her. She left immediately, and I found out there was no one else home. I lay there for about three hours until my wife came home, and I learned a very important lesson in timing.

The reason I wrote this chapter is so people would know about the side they don't usually see. So when you see somebody in a wheelchair, you can now know that there's a secret life known mainly to their caregivers, family, and a few friends. Most people don't realize that the girl they see pushing me around town in the wheelchair is doing things behind the scenes that make her one of the hardest working, most valuable, and smartest people in the work force. When I have somebody really good in this position, it makes my life a lot easier, and I get a lot more work done each day. Caregivers are the least recognized, least complimented, and most unappreciated people in the workforce. I've said it before, and I'll say it again; when you are visiting a person with a disability make sure you compliment the caregiver, ask them how they're doing, and if you're in a position to do so, ask them if they could use a break. Asking them if they need a break applies more to family caregivers. I want to thank all the caregivers who have helped me over the last twenty-four years. Without every one of you, I would not have made it this far. It's a team effort. I know some of the members of the team weren't so happy with the job, and for you, I'm sorry. But for most of you, it worked out well for both of us. Many of you, and you know who you are, became such close friends that I think of you almost as daughters. A lot of you still come to visit, and I still see others as I'm out and about. I hope life is treating all of you well, and if you're ever in Fargo, please come to visit.

Even if it's tough to continually hire new employees and the cost is prohibitive, it's still worth it. The alternative for me is to go to a nursing home. I would then lose control of my life because they would get me up on their schedule, feed me on their schedule, and put me to bed on their schedule. I also wouldn't have the freedom to come and go as I please or to have people over to my house for meals, to visit, or watch TV. I wouldn't be able to work and have the dream that something I do will hit big and that I will be financially independent again. In the nursing home, people lose their dreams, which in my case keep me going. Many times, my dreams seem unattainable. But as long as I know there's a chance, I can keep working hard. This goes back to the whole concept of the book. Working hard and overcoming obstacles to success is what makes the days go fast and raises low self-esteem to high self-esteem. It is true that at times, when things aren't going well, the thought of giving up and taking what appears to be the easy way by going into the nursing home enters my mind. But I know that it's not the easy way and that in the nursing home my mind would deteriorate and my attitude and self-esteem would be at an all-time low. People would not be calling me for inspirational purposes. As long as I can, I'm going to continue to take the route that appears to be the hard way out but is ultimately the easy way out.

Chapter 10

ATTENDANTS, SECRETARIES, NURSES, COOKS, AND CHAUFFEURS

The people who work for me perform all of the duties listed in the title of this chapter and many more. Working for me requires common sense, the ability to learn a lot of different tasks, and the patience and skill to have multiple projects going at one time. The most important part of the job is working well with me. If we don't like each other or enjoy each other's company, it will not be a pleasant environment, and the job won't work. Throughout the years, I've learned that my hidden handicaps and how my employees react to my hidden handicaps determine how well we get along. It took me awhile to learn this, but since then, I've come to realize just how important hidden handicaps are in our work relationships as well as our personal relationships. I guess that shouldn't surprise me, and it shouldn't surprise you either.

Part of the reason I didn't realize this early on is that I didn't have as many people working for me then as I do now. In fact, my employee situation started out much like a normal workweek. In the beginning, we had attendants who worked eight to five, Monday through Friday and eight to noon on Saturday. My wife and children took care of me the rest of the time. After awhile, my employee situation started requiring more and more hours. After two years, we hired a girl to live in our home. She would put me to bed each night at ten and then would be on call during the night until the girl on the dayshift came at eight in the morning. The live-in girl worked Sunday night through Thursday night. The family still took care of me during the evenings, Friday and Saturday overnight, and all day Sunday. As my children started moving out, we hired two girls to live in our home and take care of me fifteen nights a month each. We also hired girls to work five to ten in the evenings, all day Saturday, and all day Sunday. We now had people covering all the shifts twenty-four hours a day, seven days a week. When you have people working for and with you all the time, those relationships play a pretty significant role in your life.

Over the years, I have employed between three hundred and four hundred workers. The majority of them worked a period of eight months to one and a half years. However, some of them worked for me for years. The person who has the longest record working for me is Liz Fevig-Hager; she worked more than eleven years. Linda Olson worked for me for eight years, Denise Zastoupal worked seven years, and Mary Hannah Tanata has been with me for more than seven years. She now rents an apartment in the upper level of the home and only helps out once in awhile, since she has graduated from college with a master's degree and has a day job. Because many of the girls have worked for me for so long, I've gotten to know many of them very well and have also developed friendships with some of their families. Even after they no longer work for me, many of them come back to visit, and/or we talk on the phone. However, this is not always the case.

After my accident, I had a lot of hidden handicaps, many of which I have talked about. For the purpose of getting along with my employees, the worst three were anger, pent-up frustration from all my losses, and unreasonable expectations of my employees. Some girls were not quitters, and lasted until they learned the job. Once they learned the job and we got to know each other, working relations improved immensely. However, there were girls who could not last through that first part of the job. In some cases, employees left because we didn't get along. In other cases, we got along fine, but the job was not the right one for them. Maybe they were not fast learners or maybe they could not handle my frustration and anger. My wife told me for years that when I got frustrated I had "that voice" that treated people as if they were not smart enough and showed little respect for them.

For a long time, when my wife kept telling me about "that

voice" and when she said that I was either causing girls to quit or making their lives miserable, I thought she was wrong. My defense was, "If I am so terrible, why do I get along so well with many of the girls, and why do girls stay with me seven and eight years?" It took a long time, but I finally figured it out. If I could hire a girl who was a fast learner, was a perfectionist herself, and understood that doing things my way did not mean that I thought she was stupid, then we would get along fine. The girls I got along with understood that there was more than one way to do certain things. The employee's way, which was different than mine, was just as effective as the way I did it. It was just a personal preference. Since these girls did not do the things that invoked my hidden handicaps, we got along fine. The girls with different personalities who triggered my hidden handicaps did not get along with me, and life was miserable for both of us. This did not mean that they were bad girls, nor did it mean that they weren't good workers. It simply meant that when working with them, my character flaws showed up rather dramatically.

Some workers would have done a good job had I allowed them to, some were great workers, but we didn't get along, and there were some girls who simply couldn't do the job. I would like to take this opportunity to apologize to all the girls who left my employment with bad feelings. You can all feel justified knowing that slowly, but surely, I have realized that my employment relationships that did not work out were much more my fault than the employee's. Input from my family and counseling has helped me realize this. I think that I have eliminated a lot of hidden handicaps that may have been the root of these poor relationships and that I am now an easier person to work for and get along with than I was ten, fifteen, or twenty years ago. This is one of the reasons to try to eliminate your hidden handicaps: it will make you an easier person to get along with. It will even help your working relationships.

Even if you haven't gotten rid of your hidden handicaps, just knowing what they are can help you in your work relationships. Knowing your hidden handicaps can also help you when choosing an employee, spouse, a boss, a partner, roommate, etc. If you can identify your character flaws or hidden handicaps earlier in life than

I did, then you can avoid a lot of pain and suffering. After identifying these hidden handicaps, you should work to overcome them. But sometimes it takes a long time to eliminate them, and some of them may never be eliminated completely. Now that I have identified the type of people I don't work with very well, I shouldn't hire them. They are not bad people, and they will make somebody great employees, but not me. I am a perfectionist, so I try to hire a girl who is somewhat similar. I'm not real patient with people who don't learn the job quickly, so I try to hire girls who are fast learners. If a girl has worked for me two or three weeks and I see that we're not matching up very well, I know that she's just as frustrated as I am. I talk to her about the situation and give her plenty of time to find a new job, which also gives me plenty of time to find a new employee. I'm working on a lot of changes, but I have to hire people and pick other relationships based on what I am today and not on what I hope to become in the future. For example, if you were a smoker and were going to marry someone who couldn't stand smoking, you wouldn't want to do it on the basis that you were going to quit smoking because if you didn't quit, it would be a disaster. My advice to all of you is to work hard to identify your hidden handicaps. It is important to work at getting rid of these handicaps, but until you do, it can be very helpful in the choices that you have to make everyday. Some of these choices will fit in with your hidden handicaps, and others will be a big mistake because of your character flaws.

In order to demonstrate how hidden handicaps can affect work relationships, Mary Hannah Tanata and I chose seven girls, who have worked for me, who we thought were good representatives of the last twenty-four years of my journey. They are also among the elite of all of the girls who have ever worked for me, but I easily could list another fifty who would fall into that group. We asked these seven girls to write a story about how it was to work for me. Obviously, these are girls whom I got along with because they were able to accept my hidden handicaps. I asked some girls whom I hadn't gotten along with to write a story, but none of them would do it. The fact of the matter is my hiring of these seven girls was luck because when I hired them, I had not identified most of my hidden handicaps and was in denial about the ones that I knew about. I wrote a little bit about each girl before I read her story so that I would not be influenced by what she said. I'm hoping that you will be able to see how my hidden handicaps affected our relationships, even though my hidden handicaps didn't destroy the relationships.

I put these stories in order of when the girls worked for me just to see if there would be a change in the types of relationships once I started working on my hidden handicaps. The order of these attendants' stories is not by talent, as they were all equally talented in their own ways. The first five girls worked for me after I became aware of some of my hidden handicaps, but before I was doing anything about them.

Linda Olson worked for me before any of the other girls. Linda is a quiet, extremely efficient, sweet person. She was also tied with several other girls as the best cooks I ever had. Linda didn't like my gambling hidden handicap, so I tried to have her hold my cards as little as possible. Linda was almost as crazy as Liz was, as she worked part time for me for approximately eight years. Linda worked for me while most of the kids were still at home, and she made many evening meals before she left at five. All the kids remember Linda's chicken chow mein, homemade wontons, and sweet and sour sauce, as well as her tomato, green pepper steak. Linda was also an LPN. Linda has a very nice husband named Bob, a computer whiz who used to put programs on my computer and fix it when it went wacky. Linda and Bob moved out of town, or Linda might have gotten her twenty-year watch. I still talk to the two of them several times a year. They have been very good to me since they left and have helped me on many occasions.

Linda's version . . .

My youngest daughter Nicole was only a few months old when I started working for Tom in 1981; Nicole is now twenty years old. I worked part-time through 1989 and have only seen Tom a couple of times since then, as we moved out of the Fargo-Moorhead area. Even though it has been several years since I worked for Tom, I have many memories of the experience.

I did not know Tom before his accident. My first impression of him was not at all what I expected. He was definitely a take-charge kind of person and definitely not the kind to sit around and feel sorry for himself. I have always had great respect for him because of that. It was amazing to see what he could accomplish. He could sell anything from insurance to drinking glasses. He worked hard everyday, which meant whoever was with him worked hard too.

Working in the Day household was a very unique experience. It was a very busy place that included five kids (who were involved in school, sports, and jobs), live-in helpers, and nurses or attendants— all coming and going at all hours. Not to mention Sam, the dog, and all the cats. Sometimes it was all a little overwhelming because it would seem that Tom would want me to be doing ten things at once. It was like he no longer had any concept of how long it takes to do certain tasks. He would even get a little impatient at times. The faster I worked, the faster he'd think of something else that needed to be done. He must keep a constant list going in his head. I guess it was his way of controlling his life. Although he was totally dependent on others for his care, he was still going to run things. He was very good at managing things; but of course, he had a lot of time to sit and think and plan.

Tom is also very generous and kind. He loved to have kids come and visit. When my daughter Heidi had chicken pox and couldn't go to school or daycare, I brought her to work with me one day. (After making sure Tom had already had the chicken pox.) Tom had Heidi dial the phone for him, and at the end of the day, he gave her $10, which was a very big deal to her at the time. She still remembers it! He was also generous to his regular workers, paying us overtime if we worked longer than we were scheduled for or if we came over for awhile on a weekend. He was very appreciative.

I guess what I liked the least about working for Tom was being with him when he was gambling. I really didn't want to be a part of it, especially when I had to sit at the poker table and hold his cards. If Mike were there, he would help Tom play cards. But then it was extremely boring for me unless someone wanted something to eat, then I would cook. I did enjoy cooking, and sometimes Tom would have me cater parties. We would plan the menu together, and then I'd go shopping and spend the day cooking. One of Tom's favorite foods for me to make was deep-fried wontons.

Tom has had many obstacles to overcome in the past twenty-some years. He has never let any of it get him down. He has never let his situation keep him from doing things. He always went to all of his kids' sporting events, and he came to my college graduation party and even Heidi's high school graduation party. He didn't just sit at home even though it might have been easier for him. It's like that popular country song says, "You can't keep a good man down."

Dawn Sowka started working for me about two years after Linda did. Dawn is really full of life. She was always positive and always smiling. She very seldom got down, and she loved my gambling hidden handicap. We always had a great time going to poker games and tournaments, but she also loved the secretarial work and was very good at it. Dawn was always able to lift up my spirits on a day when things weren't going well. As with most of the girls, I got to know her family. Her mother even worked part-time for me once in awhile. Dawn worked for me for several years. She now lives in Southern California with her children and is doing very well running a tutoring business. I still talk to Dawn on the phone eight or nine times a year. If I ever came into a lot of money, I would be calling Dawn to come back to work for me. Not that she doesn't like California, but I think she still has a warm spot in her heart for North Dakota.

Dawn's version . . .

You asked me to contribute a piece in your book, to describe what it was like to work for you. I felt honored that you asked me to do this. I hope I can complete this task without letting you down, I hope my words will be powerful enough to pay tribute to a man I have such great respect for, and I hope this will inspire others to look within themselves and to realize that we all face obstacles in our lives but that we have the choice to overcome them.

I remember the day I interviewed with you for the position of nurse/secretary. I was nervous at the prospect of a new job. I entered the house and wasn't quite sure where to turn to find you. I walked into the kitchen and was greeted by kids, groceries, dishes, half-eaten lunches on the counter, and chaos everywhere. Someone directed me to your room. After spending five minutes amidst the chaos, I no longer felt nervous, but excited at what might be in store.

I soon learned you were a man who didn't let any grass grow under his feet. You were never afraid to try new things and always had something in the works. One of my favorite memories is doing physical therapy with you, while answering the phone, while eating lunch. This was typical. Multi-tasking all day. Little did I know that you were preparing me for motherhood! The more involved I became in your life, the more impressed I was with you as a person. I was fascinated by the way you conducted your business, how you lived, and how you managed the intricate details of your days. You juggled family life, business ventures, and high stakes poker games like a ringmaster. For a person without physical limitations, directing a circus act would be daunting enough. You, however, emceed the entire performance with grace and style.

It was exhausting enough in the beginning because everything had to be explained. There was a lot for me to learn. The exhausting part wasn't in learning the secretarial responsibilities, the nursing duties, physical therapy exercises, or the insurance business. Oh no! The exhaustion was in the hours it took for you to explain the details of how to file a document in a filing system you had created, but never seen. In a job-training situation, showing the employee a filing system takes five minutes. This was impossible in your situation because your wheelchair couldn't fit through the door to the room where the filing system was. You depended on not only your fine-tuned memory but also on us following your directions explicitly. When either of these failed, your valuable time and energy was spent. For me, this was an exercise in patience, and a relationship of trust and faith was fostered.

An outsider watching you eat wouldn't appreciate the steps that had to be learned to finish a meal. First, was preparing the food just how you liked it. When you said, "Easy on the peanut butter," exactly how easy did you mean? "Easy" to me was different than "easy" to you. After several trips back to the kitchen, I learned what "easy" meant. Now onto the eating. Food had to be cut in such a way that it was easy for me to pick up and easy to feed to you as well. Then there was the order in which you liked to eat your food. Another step in the dance. After much practice, the dance was learned. We read each other's signals and performed without missing a beat. A simple task that we all do unconsciously (brushing our teeth) was once again a challenging obstacle to overcome. How difficult for you to explain that you were ready to rinse when you had a mouthful of toothpaste and a toothbrush in your mouth. I had to learn when to move to the bottom row, how much pressure to apply, and whether to move the brush up and down or in a circular motion. You had to communicate your needs, and we had to find a rhythm. Eventually I learned and could brush your teeth as easily as I brush my own. These "simple" tasks became second nature and were no longer given much attention. They could be accomplished without much thought or attention. It was at this point that the job became thrilling. We joked that my resume would be several pages long in order to include all the skills that were learned while working with you. That was one of the many things I loved about the job. We had our routine and took care of the essentials, but no two days were ever the same. Your ideas were endless. I never knew what we would be involved in when I came to work each day.

What strength you showed in enduring people being involved in every part of your life, your person. I often wondered how you did it. It should have been a humbling experience, but you never seemed to be bothered by it. I learned so many life skills working with you. I've seen you hit rock bottom and pull yourself up so many times that I have no doubt you're a survivor. Whatever life throws at you, I know you will overcome it. You made me realize that we always have a choice. Your choice has always been to pick up and move on. You've taught me to take control and make life work. You've taught me to live life to its fullest. You live with dignity and honor, and I am proud that I had the chance to work with you twenty years ago. You have had an incredible impact on me, and I am grateful for the friendship that was created and that you are involved in my life today.

Annette Hogetvedt is next on the list. I think Annette was with me off and on for about three years. She had a wonderful personality and was another great employee. I think Annette's and my sense of humor matched up about as well as anybody who worked for me. Annette and I both loved sports so that was also a common interest. She took me to many sporting events in Fargo. The thing I liked about going to games with her is that she understood the game so well that I could talk to her about the game. She also worked for me when Joe played for Moorhead State University and took me on many road trips, and we always had a good time. I would probably have to say that Annette was almost perfect except that God gave her a right foot made out of lead. Her nickname was "Annetti Andretti." When she was driving my van, there was no wear and tear on my tires, since they weren't touching the pavement! Annette recently got married to Jim McFadzen, and they live in Phoenix. I am a good friend of Annette's folks Leo and Yvette. We all wondered if Annette would find anyone who would earn Leo's approval. Jim, you must be quite a guy!

Annette's version . . .

When Tom asked me to write a little story for his book, I was a little hesitant. When I think back to the years I worked for Tom, I think we both learned a lot from each other, and I know I became more aware of people with disabilities and how to react to people with disabilities. Tom and his family influenced me, and the experience made me a better person.

By now, all you readers realize Tom is a quadriplegic. When I pulled up to Tom's driveway to interview for the job, he was sitting outside in his wheelchair sun tanning (that's what I called it). I would have never guessed that I would go to work for this guy. First of all, Tom's a big guy, even in a wheelchair. I found him quite intimidating. His pet peeve is when people don't talk directly to him. Not directing a question to a handicapped person is being ignorant yourself. I did talk to him directly; therefore, I passed the initial test. Tom figured I would probably work out. My driving ability would be questioned later, but that's a different story.

I couldn't imagine how much I would enjoy the job. I started working for Tom in the fall of 1989. I was the type of employee who lived in his home and helped out during the evenings and weekends. This was part of our job for the free room and board. Walking into someone's home and trying to fit in without alienating the original family members is difficult. I never felt comfortable living in someone else's home where privacy is limited. I understood that this is the only way Tom could live at home, yet for the rest of the family, it meant having strangers in a home where they could never run around naked if they wanted to (I'm not saying they wanted to). Being an only child myself, I understand the privacy issue and the need for space. That's probably why later I moved into my own apartment by myself but continued to work for Tom.

Getting to know Tom was interesting. The first thing I learned was that no matter what, you do it his way. Even if you have a different, better, or quicker way, you do it his way since he is paying you. I think back on how quirky it was that he had to have spaghetti made a certain way or his hair washed a certain way. What difference did it make? It made a lot of difference. For someone who could not do the things himself, he wanted it done just like he would do it. Thus, you adapted to how he wanted things done. I liked to cook, and that part of the job was a breeze.

When I worked for Tom, he was selling. It didn't matter if it was water purification units or if it was trying to sell himself. His job was/is selling. The funny thing is Tom does things most normal people wouldn't even try. Nothing is impossible for Tom, especially when it comes to trying to get something accomplished. On business trips, most people have the luxury to be able to stay in hotels and drive wherever they desire. When Tom planned a business trip, it might have also involved a football game, but that's just good planning. We once drove from Fargo, North Dakota to Lincoln, Nebraska to visit Pure Water and then on to Kearney, Nebraska to watch his son play football. Then we left and drove back to Fargo. We managed to accomplish this in one day. Most normal people wouldn't even try that. I can't imagine ever doing that again. If Tom didn't have his handicap, I'll guarantee he wouldn't have done it that way, but he didn't have any other choice.

Tom has always had people living in his house with him to help at night. When you have a need for twenty-four-hour care, you do have a few people around all the time to help out. Tom would always try to make things as comfortable for us as possible. He didn't think it was fun having to get someone up in the middle of the night to adjust something on the bed, move the heat lamp, or scratch an itch. It's things like that that we take for granted. Tom doesn't take those things for granted. He has to figure out a way to get all those little things accomplished. Tom manages to get things accomplished, no matter if it's making next month's mortgage payment or finding his next employee. He finds a way to accomplish his goals.

Tom is genuinely a really nice guy. He's in control of his life as much as he can be, but he relies on the people working for him to make sure everything is okay. How do you trust someone with your health, finances, home, vehicle, everything, including your life? That takes a mutual trust between the two people. When I moved out from living at the house and into my own apartment, I still did work for Tom and helped him out every now and then. But I was becoming more independent, and I had started a different job. I knew that I wouldn't be able to do this for the long haul, and I didn't want to be tied down. You can't tell someone who is counting on you to come to work, "No thanks, I have other plans." The biggest problem was that I couldn't tell Tom no; therefore, I found it easier to not commit to working at all. Sounds typical for a young adult. That's exactly why I ended up having to write a little brief in his book. I couldn't tell him no. It's not a matter of pity when helping him; it's a matter of wanting to help someone who is genuine and kind, but what he needs is to be able to do things for himself again, and no one can give him that.

Mary Hannah Tanata has worked for me off and on for the last seven years. Hannah has the record for moving out and moving back in. She has done it five times. She is like one of the family.

Hannah is helping me with this book by doing a lot of the editing and working with the other attendants and helping them with their stories. One of the reasons that Hannah and I get along is that she's a perfectionist too, although I would imagine that my hidden handicap of anger bothers her. Hannah grew up on a farm and has a wonderful set of parents and a very nice brother. A lot of the girls who have worked for me have grown up on farms. They know how to work, and they usually have a lot of common sense. That doesn't mean there aren't a lot of great gals who grew up in the city, but percentage wise, I have not had many girls who grew up on a farm who didn't succeed at this job. Mary Hannah ties Linda Olson as being the best cook I've ever had. When I invite guests over, she serves them a gourmet meal and can do it in record time. Hannah has moved into an apartment on our second floor. We've had a lot more home-cooked meals since she moved in.

Mary Hannah's version . . .

In January of 1995, I was attending school at North Dakota State University. In dire need of spending money, I responded to an ad in the paper for a job working with a handicapped person that stated, "light duties required." The day of my interview was the first time I met Thomas J. Day; and upon meeting me, he hired me on the spot. Flattered and not fully understanding the intensity of the "light duties," I accepted.

January 27th, 1995 was my first day of work for Thomas J. (which I affectionately call him now). The first night, Dave Drenth took Tom to play poker. He left me to do some cleaning in the house, so that night went fine. My "light duties" for the next night were to get Thomas J. ready for an NDSU Bison basketball game, drive him there, attend the game, and bring him home to put him to bed. No big deal, right? Wrong. It was 30° below zero, and we were late for the game (later I discovered that we would always be late). I had never put Tom into the van in the wheelchair lift or hooked his wheelchair up in the van. I had also never driven the van. Tom kept telling me to hurry, which was difficult when everything was so new. When we got to the Bison Sports Arena, there was no handicapped parking, so I had to park by the ramp and take Tom into the game and get him situated to watch the game. By this time, I was a nervous wreck. I went back outside to park the van, but there was no place to park on the south side of the building. The parking attendant told me to drive around to the north end of the building to find a parking spot. I drove over there and finally found a spot to park. I sat in the van for awhile and cried and wondered how I possibly thought, at eighteen, that I could be responsible for another person.

By the time I got back into the gym, it had been more than a half an hour, and Tom asked, "Where have you been? I wondered what had happened to you, and I was going to send someone out to look for you." The rest of the night went all right, but I didn't think I could handle this job. After that night, I called in sick for two weeks. It must have been fate that Thomas J. didn't get rid of me after not showing. The reason I came back is I realized I had to quit or go to work, and I've never been a good quitter. I guess at this point you could say, "The rest is history."

Throughout the last seven years, Thomas J. and I have been together during good times and bad times. It is a relationship that has taught me many great values and lessons. I wonder now what I would be like and where I would be if I would have decided to quit that February. However, this story is not to help you understand the growth that I have achieved knowing Thomas J., but the growth that I have experienced Thomas J. go through in the time I have known him.

I have known for a long time that Thomas J. has a golden heart, an amazing mind, and a strong will. The greatest of all growth I have seen in Thomas J. is the fact that he believes in himself and the true gifts of life so much that he now shows this amazing person I have seen inside him.

Thomas J. is now part of my family and everyday life. I love him like I love my father, and I consider his friends and family my own. We live, laugh, and love together and have a relationship that I will forever be thankful for. Congratulations, Thomas J., on your discovery of the wonderful person you can be, and thank you for the wonderful experience and awareness you have given a small town

18-year-old who only wanted to make some spending money doing
"light duties."

The day Kristi Alm-Pagel came to interview for the attendant/
secretary job, we had so many applicants that my daughter Mo and a
girl who was working for me were helping me interview. Mo and the
other girl would screen the applicants and would only send back the
ones they thought would be good. After Mo got done interviewing
Kristi, she came back and said to me, "Hire her." It's a long story, but
I had some difficulty getting Kristi to come work for me. I finally
managed to talk her into it, and she was another tremendous employee.
About the only problem Kristi and I had was that we were both hard
headed, so we had to communicate to arrive at a mutual agreement.
My gambling hidden handicap didn't bother Kristi. She loved to
take me to poker games and tournaments. We both loved the casino
atmosphere! Since I quit gambling four and a half years ago, those
days are gone forever. Kristi and I still remain good friends, as I do
with all the girls in this chapter.

Kristi's version . . .
What can I say about Tom Day? Well, let me give you a little
history of our relationship that will help you understand my perception
of him. I first met Tom through an ad in the paper. His daughter, Mo,
interviewed me. I must have passed that test because she wanted me
to meet him. I had no idea what to expect when I walked down that
hall to Tom's room. Of course, how could I? I met with Tom, and
although he seemed gruff, we seemed to get along well from the
beginning. I started working for Tom, and a couple of days later, I
received an offer from another company that I had interviewed with
at about the same time. I decided to take that position since it had
benefits, and honestly, I didn't know if the fast-paced life that Tom
led was for me. After several attempts to get a hold of him over the
weekend, I decided to leave him a message. I explained that I had
taken another position, that it was nice meeting him, and that I wished
him the best. I thought that was the end of Tom Day as far as I was
concerned . . . I was wrong. When I returned home that evening, my

now husband, Dave, told me Tom had called and wanted me to call him back. Then he looked me square in the eyes and said, "I don't think he's done with you yet." He couldn't have been more right. I called Tom, and the best salesman I have ever known talked me into coming back. I liked Tom, but I barely knew him then. This was my first experience with the one-of-a-kind determination and persistence that I would grow to admire in Tom. I believe that those two elements have been key to his independence and his survival.

I spent an enormous amount of time with Tom while we worked together. I got him up in the morning (sometimes faster than others), drove him to meetings, appointments, lunches, etc. We made phone calls, had meetings, and went on sales calls. He was the brain of the operation (there's no doubt about that); I simply acted as his hands and did for him the things he could no longer do for himself. Most days we had a good time together. We have many similarities, but our brutal honesty is probably what enabled us to work so well together. I told him what I saw, good or bad, with absolutely no sugar coating. I never felt sorry for Tom. He's more of a man than most men walking on the streets. And on the days he had a tough time keeping on, I tried to make him see the good things. And in exchange, Tom told me how he wanted things done, precisely. He is definitely a creature of habit. His routine allows him to feel that he has a reasonable amount of control over his world. I understood that and didn't fight it . . . much.

One of the other things I spent a lot of time doing with Tom was gambling. We went and played cards two, sometimes three, times a week. I'd hold his cards, practice my poker face, and eventually I learned the games, although not very well, looking back. We drove to tournaments at casinos sometimes states away. Some nights, when the cards were good to us, we had a great time. On the other nights, and there were plenty of them, the drives home were long and quiet. Sometimes, I could see the change in Tom when his luck would change. I knew how hard it was on him to lose, especially when he had to work so hard just to keep his head above water. The financial burdens that he's endured are unimaginable. The gambling was an escape for him—time that he didn't have to deal with reality. Sometimes the return to reality was torture for Tom, for us, and for his family. Everyone close to Tom was relieved when he chose to close that chapter of his life.

I think everyone whose life has been touched by Tom has different opinions, experiences, and favorite memories of Tom. My favorite times with Tom revolve around beginnings and ends. At the beginning of summer, I loved to take Tom outside to work in the sun. He was always in a better mood when he could be outside. I love to hear his stories of growing up; hitchhiking from Detroit Lakes to Fargo, golfing, football, basketball, water-skiing . . . the list goes on and on. Mary Hannah and I would sing with Tom to Patsy Cline, Alabama, and the Statler Brothers while he'd get up in the morning and while he went to bed. Both of us called him Thomas J., and we both always kissed him on the forehead when we'd say goodnight. Tom saw us through a lot of hard times, and we did our best for him.

Although Thomas J. definitely has his faults (he's demanding, can have a short temper, yells sometimes when he doesn't need to, and likes what he likes), he is much more good than bad. Tom taught me so much about life. He taught me that persistence is the key to success. He taught me that the easy way isn't always the best way. He taught me that you can't judge people by their appearance, and if you chose to, you will never see anything more than the surface. You will miss wonderful people with much to give because you are scared, shallow, or ignorant. None of these things are acceptable, and Tom will tell you so. I'll second it. He taught me that sometimes you have to cut ties to people, habits, and dreams to survive. He taught me that although money is important for necessities, you can make it with little to spare if you have to. He taught me that friendship is invaluable. He taught me that happiness is very hard to find, and if you find it, hang on to it; you deserve it. He taught me that forgiveness may take time, but if you can forgive someone you care about, it's yourself you set free. He taught me that everyday is a gift from God that should never be taken for granted. Most of all, he taught me about the kind of person I want to be.

Thomas J. is more than my old boss. He is my friend, part of my family. And even though I don't see him everyday anymore, I *think of him often. I am grateful that I was able to be a part of his life, and he mine. I am most grateful that I had the opportunity to be his student in the game of life. I love you Thomas J. Thank you for calling me back!*

Benita Greff, whom I hired after starting to overcome my hidden handicaps, had gone to school with a girl who was living here. That girl asked me if I wanted to interview Benita, as we had an opening for a live-in. What a lucky break that was. Benita was one of the best live-ins I ever had. She was smart, efficient, always on time, and very dependable. Benita's efficiency complimented my hidden handicap of perfectionism very well. However, I had trouble getting Benita to communicate when I knew that something was wrong, which drove me crazy at times. When there were shifts that couldn't be filled, Benita was one who would always take them. She was also good about trading shifts with the other girls when they had conflicts. Benita is a Catholic, and she and I enjoyed going to Mass together. I am a very sarcastic person, but I can't hold a candle to Benita Greff. She had a very sharp tongue, but she was such a nice girl that she never wanted to hurt anybody's feelings, so right after she gave you a zinger, she would say, "Just kidding." There were two other girls living here at the same time as Benita named Theresa and Rhonda. They were almost as sarcastic as Benita, and as you listened to the three of them talk, you would continually hear "Just kidding," "Just kidding," "Just kidding." After Benita moved out, because of her internship, she still came back and filled in for me when there was an open shift. She would also sign up for shifts at the beginning of the month when she knew we were going to be short. Benita also helped me during the early stages of writing this book. She is very good at writing. I have not read her story, but I assume it will have one or two sarcastic remarks in it.

Benita's version . . .

I only worked as one of Tom's attendants for one-and-a-half years; but in that time period I learned much about myself and even more about how to live. Working for Tom was challenging, rewarding, and, at times, frustrating.

The most important part of my job was maintaining a positive relationship with Tom. From my first day of work, Tom and I became friends. He liked my smart-aleck comments, and I liked his off-the-wall stories. I was inspired by his determination to succeed despite the obstacles life had presented him. As I continued to work with him, I always respected his determination, but I also faced some challenging time periods. After about nine months of working for Tom, I faced a time period when I was about to call it quits. At the time, I had a full load of homework every night, Tom was sick, and we were short-staffed. For a couple of months, another attendant and I split the evening and overnight shifts, and usually worked three out of four weekends in a month. I felt good about helping Tom, but I was feeling the stress and starting to get a bad attitude. While Tom was sick, he woke us up to get him water, blow his nose, take his temperature, and shake his knees (a method used to get blood flowing through his body when he is feeling light-headed) many more times than was normal. During some of my overnight shifts, Tom woke me up on the hour, every hour, for the duration of the shift. A few mornings, I went to school with only three to four hours of sleep.

I strove to maintain a positive attitude. When I first began, Liz, one of Tom's full-time attendants, told me she thought of herself as Tom's hands and feet. Her job was to make Tom independent through the use of her able-bodied capabilities. Realizing this made her immune to feeling offended by all Tom asked her to do. When Tom wanted toast cut diagonally instead of vertically, she didn't take it personally. Tom was using her as an instrument to perform mundane tasks to his preferences – and it was her job to try to comply. I tried to adopt Liz's attitude; I tried to be patient; I tried to remind myself that Tom was sick and feeling terrible. But I felt overworked. My own bad attitude was reflected in how Tom treated me. I started talking less during my shifts, and Tom did too, and during many overnights, I was very short with Tom. At times, I was rude.

After many nights, my bad attitude reached its peak when, after Tom would call my name to wake me up in my room across the hall, I would lie still hoping he would decide he didn't need help before finally "hearing" him on the second or third call. I hated feeling annoyed and discouraged, but I didn't do anything to make it better. I just told myself that I would get over it. One night, I did get over it. I was especially rude to Tom, and he asked if he had done anything to make me mad. I told Tom I was fine, but he wouldn't accept "fine" as an answer. I had made my frustrations very visible. I told him exactly how stressed out I was and that I couldn't recapture my good feelings about working for him. He told me that he had been struggling to get a positive mindset himself. Our moods had been feeding off of each other.

After talking to Tom, the overnights became easier. When I was in a bad mood, I did my best to squelch it, and Tom did the same. I also let Tom know when I had a tough day. After a few days, I didn't have to struggle any more. My good feelings were back, and more easily maintained. Working hour upon hour in close proximity with another person is demanding and takes mutual respect and courtesy. A successful work environment in these circumstances requires honesty with the boss. In many environments, confiding in a boss is unprofessional, but when I worked for Tom, confiding in my boss was imperative.

I left Tom to take an internship in my field, but I am glad I left on good terms. I am glad I didn't quit while I was frustrated with work because I like to maintain my ties to Tom. After my time working for him, I am still very inspired by Tom's determination to live an independent life and by his constant struggle to better himself. Sure, Tom has his ups and downs like anyone, but each down is higher than the last, and each down comes less frequently than the low-points Tom has experienced before. I learned a lot through my own experience working for Tom, but I also learned a lot through Tom's experiences. I hope to use his wisdom to help make better decisions in my life.

My most recent employee of these seven is Angi Simonson. At the present time, Angi is my full-time day person. She works from five minutes after eight to five minutes after five, Monday through Friday. Angi started three years ago as a live-in and also worked the part-time hours. Angi has an older sister who has cerebral palsy, so she has always made me feel good when she is helping me. I have always liked Angi, but when she first came to work for me, she would sometimes be a little undependable. She wasn't anxious to switch shifts with the other girls, although she would at times, and she also wasn't anxious to work extra hours. Angi was excellent at her job, and most of the time we got along fine, but we did have several times where we had our differences. In the summer of her first year, Angi went back to her hometown. I didn't think she'd come back to work the next fall because she was also working part-time for a quadriplegic friend of mine. She went back to work for him in the fall, and she helped us out when we were short. In 2001, Angi continued to work for me on a part-time basis. Liz quit in October of 2000, and the woman I replaced her with decided four or five months down the road that the job was not for her. Angi, who had just graduated from college, said she would work full time for me April, May, and June. That would give me three months to try and find another full-time person. Angi was doing so well with the full-time job that I gave her a raise in May. In June, I told her if she would commit to working for me for another year, I would give her a large raise that would give her an income higher than she would make as a teacher. She said she'd do it. Angi is excellent in all facets of the job. She fills in on nights and weekends when I can't get anyone else to work. She trades shifts with the other girls. When we have to make out-of-town trips, she works seventeen- and eighteen-hour shifts, just like Liz used to do. All my friends love her, and I look forward to her coming to work every morning.

Angi's version . . .

Working for Tom Day has been anything but predictable. It's hard to say what we're doing from one day to the next. Tom has a tendency to decide at the spur of the moment to take off and go somewhere, like Grand Forks. Those are the fun days. I've been working for Tom full-time since April, and I still don't know what each day is going to hold until that morning, and even then it's unpredictable. It generally seems like there are several fires to put out before the day even starts.

I started out as a live-in, like many of his full-time girls do. I worked for Tom for almost two and a half years before taking the full-time position. Working full time is completely different than being a live-in. When I was a live-in, in January of 1999, there were a total of eleven people including Tom's son (Tim) and his wife (Ramelle), their two twins who were just born and two little girls (who were all under four), three live-ins, one basset hound with an attitude, and Tom, of course, crammed into his house. Let me tell you, that was interesting. Never a dull moment!

One of the more exciting times that I remember was going to an athletic event and coming out a few minutes before the game was over to warm up the van. It didn't start. To make matters worse, Tom was not feeling well and wanted Ready Wheels, a service provided by the ambulance service, to come pick him up and take him home. Luckily, Tom knows everyone, so there are always friends around to help keep things relaxed, which is almost always needed. Not getting the van started happened one too many times for me. Finally, after five or so trips to the mechanic, we finally figured out the trick to getting it started. Apparently, the shifter is very touchy and needs to be in just the right position. All you need to do is jiggle it! That would have been nice to figure out a long time ago.

I didn't have a hard time deciding whether or not I personally could do the job. Having grown up with a sister with a disability, helping someone do things is second nature to me. Taking care of Tom is very easy. The hardest part of the job is getting along, having patience for each other, and getting used to his lingo. "Go get that file so I can call that lady back," or "Quick push the button," are some of the phrases that we hear during our shifts. "What exactly does he mean?" I think to myself. Most of the time, I can figure out what he needs by taking a step back and thinking about what projects or paperwork we've been working on that day. However, sometimes I'm required to ask him to tell me again or to be more specific with his request—and I know how much he loves that. I think many of us would describe his directions as about as clear as mud. Sometimes I wonder if he's doing it intentionally, but then I realize it's just old age! Just kidding, Tom.

All kidding aside, working for Tom has been a great experience, definitely an experience. I, like the other girls, have gotten to meet some of the nicest, most interesting people whom we never would have met at another job. On occasion, I've forgotten that I'm working because of something we're doing. It's hard to remember you're getting paid when you're sitting at a Timberwolves or Bison game, or at church for that matter. I have learned many things from Tom and the multiple professions that he is involved in. If I ever decided to go into sales of any kind (car, health, life), I know who to call to get the proper training. Overall, my experience with Tom has opened my eyes to so many things that most people never experience.

The purpose of these stories is to show how my hidden handicaps affected others from their perception, not mine, so that you can see the stress that hidden handicaps can put on work relationships. All the girls were honest, and I appreciate that. Obviously, my hidden handicaps affected them. You heard them mention several times my perfectionist nature, my impatience, and my sharp tongue, not to mention my gambling. They each dealt with these hidden handicaps in their own way. Mostly, I think they dealt with my hidden handicaps through empathy and focusing on my positive traits. Although I'm aware of my shortcomings now, I didn't always realize when I was doing things that would irritate people. I would find out when we had talks, and that's why it was always easier to deal with someone who would tell me what was bothering them. I remember some of the talks I had with these girls that kept things going smoother than they would have gone without the communication. These girls were able to work for me for a relatively long period of time because they didn't do a lot of the things that bothered me, and when I did something that bothered them, most of the time they could overlook it or tell me about it. I admit I'm a handful, and everything these girls said is true. It seems that, even with all the ups and downs, they all left liking and admiring me. I feel the same way about all of them.

An important realization came to me from reading their stories.

I thank Annette for bringing up the fact that it was hard to say no to me. I have been selling all of my life, and when you sell, you are taught not to take no for an answer. But there is a time when you should take no for an answer, and I have a tendency to step across that line. When you are trying to sell a friend on doing something for you, that line comes more quickly. A person shouldn't have to say no very many times to have you stop asking them to do whatever it is that you are trying to get them to do. This is a hidden handicap that I have been working hard on, but I don't seem to be getting much better. Thanks again, Annette, for bringing this up.

Benita also brought up something that helps me and should help us all. I knew Benita was in overload, but I had no idea that it was quite as bad as it was. I knew something was wrong, so I really encouraged her to talk to me. She finally did, and we got a lot of things out in the open. Once you've talked, nothing seems as bad anymore. After we talked, I understood her stress level. So when I saw she was having a tough day and was behind in her schoolwork, I would give her some time to study while she was on the job. In return, she showed more patience when I was having a bad day. We parted as good friends, and that makes me happy too.

This chapter displays a lot of my hidden handicaps mixed in with a lot of friendship and love. This just proves how important it is to find people who can understand your hidden handicaps or at least tolerate them until you can overcome them. As great as these relationships are, they would be even better if the girls didn't have to look past some of my hidden handicaps. The same is true of the work and personal relationships in your life. Even though these girls were able to work with me, there were many who weren't. You don't want to risk being as lucky as I have been to find such great employees and terrific people. Take stock of your hidden handicaps, work to overcome them, and in the meantime, choose people who will understand your battle to overcome them. You heard how close I came to losing some of my best employees—people who became some of my best friends. Don't risk that!

Chapter 11

EVERYONE SHOULD WRITE A BOOK

I used to think that people wrote books because they already knew about a topic inside and out. However, writing this book taught me a lot. Yes, I already knew that I had hidden handicaps and what they were, but in talking with other people, listening to their hidden handicaps, and thinking about my own, I learned quite a bit. I became clearer on what my hidden handicaps were and, in some cases, moved from the denial stage to the resistance stage. But perhaps most importantly, in researching this book and talking with my brothers, I learned the source of many of my hidden handicaps. Hidden handicaps usually get handed down from generation to generation. Writing your own book, or at least researching it, could help you understand your hidden handicaps better and keep you from passing them on to your children. I wish I had understood them sooner so that I could have prevented the pain I caused my wife and children.

Lynda and I had more differences than similarities, which caused problems in our marriage. I could have been a lot more understanding about our differences because Lynda met me more than half way. Lynda had grown up in a happy family and didn't understand someone who had a lot of anger. Lynda was very liberal, whereas I was pretty conservative. I grew up in a family where my dad was a gambler, and my brothers and I were playing poker and betting on games when we were eleven and twelve years old. There was no gambling in Lynda's family. However, we did have some similarities. Both of our folks were very strong Catholics, and so were Lynda and I. We both loved athletics, with tennis being our greatest, mutual love. For our first date, we went to a lighted court at two in the morning for a tennis match, and I beat her. She ran to my car, locked the doors, and wouldn't let me in for about five minutes. The very last set of tennis we played, several days before my accident, she beat me.

From the very start of our marriage, Lynda and I had a lot of fights. I always thought they were either her fault or both of ours, but never mine. After going through a lot of counseling and reflecting on my own childhood, I know the fights were my fault. I also fought with my children. I would get angry with them for little or no reason, and they would always have to admit that they were wrong. I had a lot of anger, but I really didn't understand it, nor did I know why little things would set it off. I would be all right for a few days, but then some little thing that my wife or my children did would trigger it. I would scream at my wife and children about who was right until I won the argument or until it was a stalemate. I always felt bad after this happened and would usually apologize to Lynda and/or the kids. But the damage was being done. My anger and behavior caused my children to resent me. Their resentment kept growing and growing. Fortunately, I at least told them I loved them, hugged them, and played games with them to show them I cared. This was probably the denial stage of my hidden handicap. I knew there was a problem, but I was in denial about the extent it was affecting our family.

Not only was I getting angry for the tiniest of reasons, I was also gone an excessive amount of time. During the summer of the first part of our marriage, I played softball twice a week and a tournament almost every Sunday. The last ten years before my accident, I took up golf and played almost every day. In the winter, I played tennis several times a week on indoor courts. Added to that were many nights of poker and drinks with the fellows after golf, tennis, or work. Squeezed in between these activities was work. I spent approximately fifty to sixty hours doing personal sales and training my agents. I also went to many athletic events and would take some of the children or Lynda to those events. However, Lynda and the kids were all developing hidden handicaps because of mine. This is what usually happens in dysfunctional families. One person has a problem, but it causes problems for every other family member. As my children became young adults, they started telling me some of the things I had done that hurt them psychologically. Lynda had been telling me for years how I was hurting her and the kids. All that time, I was in denial and didn't believe it was that bad.

I did tell my wife and my children that I loved them, but my actions didn't match my words. I knew I was angry, but since I wouldn't go to counseling to find out what was causing the anger, I couldn't seem to change. Apparently, I got rid of most of my hostility at home. I had a lot of friends, and my children couldn't understand why I treated my friends better than my family. When Lynda would tell me how terrible I was to her and the kids, the fact that I had so many good friends confused me. I couldn't understand how I could have *any* friends if I was as bad as she said I was. It took a lot of counseling and many talks with my children to figure out what Lynda had been trying to tell me.

In 1990, because of my depression caused by the rebating incident where I lost my insurance licenses, I started going to counseling. I have been going to counseling once a week for more than ten years. Through counseling, I started understanding my anger and how destructive it had been. I also started realizing how right my wife and children had been about how I had treated them. Five years ago, I quit gambling. Once I started counseling, it took me seven years to admit that I had a problem. After I had quit gambling for awhile, I was able to look back with a clear head and realize how much my gambling had hurt Lynda as well as my relationships with my children. I finally understood how dysfunctional I was as a parent and a husband.

When I quit gambling, I went to my ex-wife and all my children, and told them how sorry I was for all the hurt my gambling had caused them. My gambling had caused many more problems for my family than I had realized. First, there was the financial damage. As I said when I first explained this hidden handicap, when I lost, the money came out of our budget or was put on a credit card. However, when I won, the money disappeared, and I usually didn't have the money to pay off the next loss. In addition to the financial damage, my gambling also caused emotional and psychological damage. When I lost, I came home and took it out on the family. Also, at one time or another, all of my kids held my cards for me when I was playing poker. Many times when I lost a pot, I would blame it on them. My son, Mike, held my cards the most. He suffered so much stress that the pain affected him physically and mentally. Mike knew that I loved him, and he couldn't figure out why I would be so mean to him. I'm sure the other kids felt this way also. None of the kids should have dealt or held my cards for me. It was insane.

After I was able to understand what I had done to my family, I was able to talk to my children on a more meaningful basis. They were able to tell me the pain and suffering my actions had caused. For example, they told me that my fights with Lynda caused them all a lot of suffering. They also said that they were all afraid to bring their friends home because of my anger. They never knew when I was going to blow up. They also told me that they all wanted me to see the good in them instead of criticizing them for what they did wrong. Many times, they hadn't done anything wrong, but I would scream at them until they would admit that they had done things that they really hadn't.

All of the kids developed their own hidden handicaps because of having to deal with mine while growing up. In talking to each one individually and realizing how much I hurt them, I asked them how they could still love me. They said because in many ways I was a good father and because they knew I loved them. They just couldn't understand why I treated them so badly at times. Their mother also kept the kids from turning against me completely. When they felt bad because of the way I was treating them and the way I was treating her, she would tell them that I was not emotionally stable. She told them that their dad loved them, but that he didn't know how to show it. She told them that my anger was part of my sickness. One of the worst things that I did to my children and wife is that I didn't witness their inner beauty and their individual talents until it was too late. †My kids have all gone to counseling and have worked very hard to put the past behind them and forgive me. I am still working hard to continue to change and earn their forgiveness. They all want to be happy and raise their families in a better environment than they grew up in. It seems like dysfunction moves from generation to generation.

My children are aware and have talked about the problems that they developed during their childhood. They are all working hard to get mentally and physically healthy. *Michael, Maureen, Kathleen, Joseph, and Timothy, I thank you all for giving me many chances to become a good father and grandfather. With your help, I've made a lot of progress. When I regress with one of you, we sometimes go backwards a little bit, but we talk and go forward again. My relationship with all of you is certainly not perfect, but I feel very close to all of you, and I think for the most part, you feel the same. Thanks again for allowing me to remain a part of your lives and your children's lives. I intend to continue to improve all of our relationships. I wish all of you love and the best possible lives for you in the future.*

As I said earlier, my wife Lynda grew up in a very loving family and was not ready for a marriage that was highlighted by anger and absence. I did a lot of things that hurt her, which are hard to forget and forgive. I'm very sorry for the way I treated her, but unfortunately I can't change any of it. I don't know why she stayed with me for seventeen years after my accident. I'm not sure if she knows either. Her staying with me saved me from going into a nursing home, and I'm very grateful. However, she would have been much better off had she left right after the accident. I think she stayed so that the children would have a father and also because her nature is to be a caregiver. Lynda left in 1994, but we still celebrate Christmas and other holidays together as a family. She is still working through her anger for the way that I treated her. *Lynda our marriage was a disaster. You kept telling me what the problems were, but I was in denial. In fact, I was so dumb that at times I thought we had a pretty good marriage. I now realize how terrible it was for you. You kept telling me how you needed to be treated, and I didn't treat you that way. After all these years, I have finally figured out that if a person says this is the way I need to be treated, then if you love them, that's the way you treat them. I wish I could wave a magic wand and change the past, but I can't. I apologize to you for every single thing I did to hurt you, and I hope that you have peace and happiness in your life.*

Even after I was finally able to admit that my anger was a

problem and had caused a lot of hurt for my family, I still hadn't figured out why I had so much anger. About five years into my counseling, I started to figure out the source of my anger and some of my other hidden handicaps. Counseling and doing research for this book raised a lot of questions about my childhood family. To get answers for these questions, I wanted to talk to my younger brothers, Bill and Pat, about how it was for them growing up in our family. Once when Bill came to visit me, we had a discussion about our childhood that we had never had before. During our conversation, Bill asked me if Dad had ever said he loved me. I had to think for awhile because I had never thought about it before. After a moment, I said, "No." Bill said, "He never told me either." Bill had been aware of this when he was younger, whereas I had not. When Bill was about fifteen years old, he went to talk to Dad with great apprehension and fear. He asked, "Dad, what do you think of me? Am I worth anything? You have never told me how you feel." Dad answered, "Bill, you never cause me any trouble, and when I ask you to do something, you do it." Then he went back to reading his paper. Bill left the room crushed by Dad's unaffectionate answer. Bill had never related this story to me before this conversation.

Several days after Bill and I had talked, Bill, Pat, and I met in our hometown of Detroit Lakes, Minnesota for supper. As the three of us visited, we asked Pat if Dad had ever told him that he loved him. Pat was like me. He had never thought about it. So after thinking for a moment, he said, "No." Then we talked about a story that our mother had told to Bill. Our grandfather on my dad's side was a conductor on the railroad, so he would be gone four or five days at a time. When our dad knew that his dad was coming home, he would sit on the front steps waiting for him. He could see his dad walking when he was about three blocks away. With anticipation, he waited until his dad got to the house. Most of the time, our grandfather would walk right by his son Joe into the house without saying a word. When I heard this, I thought it was incredible. Now we understood why our dad could not tell us he loved us. If someone never feels love, then they can't express love. Not only was our father unable to say, "I love you," he was also unable to say anything close to that.

He was unable to show us in any form that he cared about us. In fact, none of the three of us ever remember him giving us a hug.

Instead of being affectionate, my father was highly critical of me. I was a very good football player, and when I came home after a game, my dad would be lying awake waiting to talk to me. When he could hear me come up the stairs, he would call me to his bedroom door. He would never say, "Good game." Instead, he would talk about my mistakes and how I could have played better. Although he would tell me about my mistakes, he told all his friends what a great athlete his son was. One night, after we played Wayzata, a suburb of Minneapolis, was particularly painful. I had scored three touchdowns and played a very good defensive game. I also had an 81-yard touchdown called back because of clipping. Without saying, "Good game," my dad brought up another run I had made. He said that if I had cut a different way, I could have scored another touchdown. I went to bed thinking, "What do I have to do to please him?" The worst of these after-game talks came my junior year. I was a starter for several games. Then I had a game where the coach kept telling me that I was missing my block on a linebacker on our bread-n-butter play. I was the right halfback in a wing-T. The other team had two linebackers where they normally only had one. I told the coach about the problem, but he would not listen to me. It was our only loss of the year, and the coach thought I was part of the reason why we lost. The next game, the coach decided to teach me a lesson. We won the game by a large score. But I not only didn't start, I didn't play in the game at all. I was the only player on the team who didn't play. I was devastated, depressed, angry, and embarrassed. When I went home that night, I was dreading what my dad would say because I knew it wouldn't make me feel better. In my wildest imagination, I could not have anticipated how terrible it was going to be. The minute I got to the top of the steps, my dad started screaming, "How could you embarrass me like that? I brought an attorney friend of mine from Fergus Falls to see you play, and you didn't even get in the game. I've never been so embarrassed in my life!" I was so hurt and at the same time so angry that I never said a word. I just went to bed. As a matter of fact, I didn't talk to my dad for almost a year. I couldn't imagine that he wouldn't say how tough it must have been on me to go from being a starter to not playing in a blowout game. He said a few more things to me in the next few days, but when I wouldn't talk to him, he stopped talking to me. I don't know how we started talking again, but I imagine my mother had something to do with it. All through my high school sports, my dad only talked about my mistakes.

While I was growing up, there were many other examples of his lack of feelings for me. One night, he reached over a friend, who was sleeping on the outside of my bed, slapped my head, and yelled at me for something. I hated to have friends over for fear that he would yell and scream and embarrass me. As my dad got older, he started to mellow out. We got along much better, but we still never talked in any depth. I always got along much better with my mother, especially when I was younger. Mother was always there for us. While I was growing up, my mother was a steady influence in the house. She was a great mother and took awfully good care of her children. She was the buffer between our father and us kids. If we had a problem, we knew we could talk to Mom about it.

Even though I fought a lot with my dad when I was growing up, I always admired him for his integrity. Whenever I would meet a friend of my father's, they would always tell me how honest he was and what a great guy he was. My dad was very sarcastic and had a great sense of humor, but he hardly ever smiled and almost never laughed. Unfortunately, he passed this trait on to me also. If you offered me a million dollars to give a smile or laugh that isn't fake, I'd still be broke. I do smile, and I do laugh at times, but I can't do so on command. I can also think something is very funny and enjoy it without laughing. This is another small hidden handicap. I hate to have people tell me jokes because sometimes I'll think it's funny but am unable to laugh. His sarcasm was always delivered with a straight face. Even though we had a lot of fights, because of the way everyone admired and liked my dad, I held him up on a pedestal, and that's why I blocked out the past. I had never consciously thought about the fact that he never told me he loved me, or my brothers. My sister said that my dad told her that he loved her. In the old days, I think it was easier for fathers to say that to their daughters.

Now I can see why my dad had trouble showing affection. His father was worse to him than he was to us. I did many of the same things to my family that my dad had done to me. Had I known when I first got married what I know now, I would have been a much better husband and father. I can't blame my behavior on my father because it was my responsibility to go to counseling and dig out the past. I knew there were problems, but instead of blaming myself, I blamed them on Lynda, and I was too stubborn and proud to seek help. When the children told me some of the things that I had done when they were young, I didn't remember some of them. I have no doubt they happened because they sound just like my experiences with my father. It seems that dysfunctional behavior passes from one generation to the next changing ever so slightly. I was better than Dad in some areas, but worse in others.

Dad, although I had a lot of fights with you when I was growing up and was angry with you then, I had blocked all that out up until about five years ago. So I really haven't been angry with you for all these years. During my counseling and my talks with my brothers, I thought about and realized the destructive behavior that I had suffered during my childhood. The way you treated me caused me hidden handicaps that were destructive to my own marriage. Just as in my case, you probably didn't realize why you acted the way you did, and you weren't as happy as you could have been. This was caused by the lack of affection shown to you by your father. As my children have told me, they still love me because I was a good father at times, and Dad, you were a good father a lot of the time. I'm sure you loved me. You just didn't know how to show it. I forgive you, and I love you, and my past has been put to rest. Now I need to work on the future and as much as possible make up for the pain that I caused my family.

To all the readers I hope to help, here's one thing you should get out of this chapter. I said this before, but it's worth saying again, if you seem to have a lot of trouble getting along with members of your family and close friends, then you should look deep inside yourself. Don't assume it's their problem. Listen to members of your family. If they're telling you that you have a problem, believe them and go to counseling. Don't take as long as I did to get help. If you can get help early and work through your hidden handicaps, you will have a much happier life, and all the people you love and who love you will benefit greatly. If you don't seek help, you will start losing your loved ones and may never get them back. I was very lucky with as much as I was able to salvage, but I hurt a lot of people along the way. I was able to salvage as much as I did because I finally admitted my hidden handicaps and asked for forgiveness from the people I had hurt. This was part of the healing process for them as well as me.

Now the title of this chapter was not meant to assume that everyone reading it was going to write a book. It was written with the hope that a lot of you might write a journal. I learned a lot about my hidden handicaps from writing this book, and I thought I knew a lot about them already from the ten years of counseling. But writing the book and talking about it with my family and friends gave me a deeper understanding of my hidden handicaps. It also solidified that I was definitely at fault for the pain in my family. I made my public apologies here in hopes that they would take away some of the pain. If this book accomplishes that, then it has been a success for me. But I want it to be a success for you too. If you want to learn about your hidden handicaps, write in a journal, go back and do some research on your own family, then go back and do some more research on your grandparents. It will answer a lot of questions for you, and it will help you to understand some of the problems that you have. When you understand them, you will be able to work your way through them and take "the easy way out." The hard way is a toss up on whether it's tougher on you or the people who care for you. Even after you have worked through your problems, you should keep a journal. One reason to write down information is to document what you have worked though just in case you are ever tempted to go back to your old habits. You can look back in your journal periodically to confirm that you have not slipped into old destructive habits. Maybe some of you will write a book. If you do, you will find it very hard, but extremely rewarding.

Chapter 12

DON'T GIVE UP, DON'T EVER GIVE UP

During my life, I have accomplished many things that most people would not have accomplished. I am not the smartest person in the world, but I am fairly smart. I am not the hardest working person in the world, but I work hard. I am creative and a good problem solver, but still not the best. Why then do I accomplish things that almost no one else would or could accomplish? It is because I try things that no one else will try. I consider this the greatest trait that I possess. Not many people even think of some of the things that I try. The people who do think of them dismiss them before trying them because they are sure they will not work. As Robert F. Kennedy said, "Only those who dare to fail greatly can ever achieve greatly." Folks, I am here to tell you that I have failed greatly, but it does not bother me because most of my failures were impossible tasks. I am not afraid to try things and fail because not trying is another form of failure. When I achieve a seemingly impossible task, I get an unbelievable high that I find hard to describe.

"Don't Give Up, Don't Ever Give Up" means that when you are trying to accomplish something, you don't just try a few things and then give up. You try everything you can think of. Most importantly, you don't think about something and discard it with the logic that it will never work. Many times you accomplish the near impossible with methods that seem illogical. You must physically and verbally make every single attempt to achieve a goal. Don't discard any ideas because someone else tells you they won't work or because you decide they won't work. You must always keep your focus on a single purpose and block out outside influence. Here again, to not give up seems to be the hard way and to give up after a few tries looks like the easy way, but it's actually the opposite. Not giving up is the easy way because of the rewards received when you succeed.

Playing sports as a young person started me on the road to never giving up. I had some very good coaches in grade school and some great coaches in high school. I learned at an early age that in order to accomplish something you have to be able to visualize it. Obviously, I didn't always win, but I always visualized winning. Even when we played sandlot basketball, football, or baseball, I always tried hard to win. I never liked losing. In high school and college, our teams won many games that were considered upsets. I was also involved in games where our team came from way behind to win. Many times, we won when the odds were stacked against us. These experiences strengthened my thought process to never give up.

After college, when I went into the life insurance business, my attitude to never give up flourished. My first year in the business, I made the million dollar round table (an international organization), which put me in the top five percent of all life insurance agents in the world. I was the first person from North Dakota to receive this honor. Once again, in order to accomplish these things, I had to believe in what I was doing, and I was not afraid to fail. I was taught, and firmly believe, that in the life insurance business, if you don't make the sale on the first closing interview, you're not going to make it by coming back a second time. You have to do everything possible to make the sale during that first closing interview. When you leave, you should never be able to say, "If I had only ..." because you should have already used up all of your ammunition.

Thirty years ago, I gave a speech at a national convention for Mutual Benefit Life. At that time, they were the eleventh largest insurance company out of seventeen hundred. After the speech, many people who I didn't know came up to me and told me what a fantastic speech it was. One couple told me that what I had said in my speech was going to change their life. Here's what I said in my speech, and this is the way that I sold insurance. On many occasions, I would be sitting at the kitchen or dining room table interviewing and attempting to sell insurance to a husband and wife who had one or more children.

Fortunately, most of the time things went smoothly, and I made the sale. But after the presentation, if the husband was telling me that he had to think about it, or he wasn't ready to buy insurance that night, I would say, "Bill, I can't leave yet. If I upset you with what I'm going to say, please ask me to leave. I have to do everything possible to try and put this insurance on your life that I feel you need. Because if something happens to you tomorrow, and you die, I don't want it on my conscience that I didn't do everything possible to make sure that you left enough money to take care of Sally and your two daughters." Then I would start talking again about the policy and what it would do for his family when he died. Forty percent of the time, this would work, and he would buy the insurance. The other sixty percent of the time, this method would fail. This was a very tough close, and when I first started doing it, it wasn't very easy to say. What made it work was that I was selfish, and everything I said was true. I didn't want to leave the house with the chance that the husband could die and that I would feel bad because I hadn't done my very best. If you really believe this, the rest is simple. When I left, I knew that I had given it my all. If something did happen to the husband, although I would certainly feel bad, I'd know there was nothing else I could've done because I hadn't given up. This thought can be used in your everyday life. When you are talking to your spouse, children, or a friend, just think: "They could die before I ever talk to them again." Think of how differently you would treat them!

One of the things we were taught in the life insurance business is that a sale is a numbers game. If you talk to enough people, you will make sales. The better you get, the higher your percentage of sales will become. Eighty percent of people who try the life insurance business fail. Most of the time, they fail because they don't talk to enough people. They give up before they have given the system a chance to work. And they also take the failures personally. I learned not to take the failures personally. After I'd been in the business for several years, my closing ratio was about sixty percent. I knew that in order to make six sales, I would have to fail four times. So when I missed a close, I didn't worry about it because I knew I was that much closer to a sale.

One of the ways you can learn to "Don't Give Up, Don't Ever Give Up" is to make sure you look at all sides of a situation. For example, with life insurance, you can't just look at how nice it would be if the husband would buy the insurance and have enough coverage to take care of his wife and children if he dies. You have to look at what happens if he doesn't buy the life insurance and dies. You have to talk about how tough things may be for his wife and children—things like a smaller house, secondhand clothes, no college for the children, or the chance that, out of desperation, the wife marries the wrong man to support her children. There's a pretty ugly scene that can be painted if the insurance is not purchased. You can use the logic that it would be better to have the insurance and not need it than the other way around.

After my accident, I was additionally motivated to sell insurance because of my desire to stay at home. For twenty-four years, I have fought tooth and nail to stay at home. It has taken all of my strength and courage to do this. It has also taken the emotional, physical, and financial help of my family and friends and some wonderful strangers. My never-give-up attitude was strongly motivated by both the positive and the negative side of this picture. On the positive side, I wanted to be in my own home. On the negative side, I had taken care of two people who were in nursing homes and visited countless relatives and friends in nursing homes and knew that I didn't want to be there. I probably knew as much as anyone could about what it's like to live in a nursing home. Believe me, I'm not condemning nursing homes. Most nursing homes are as good as they can be. But at their best, they are not home. As I've said before, you lose control of your life. You get up when they want you to and go to bed when they want you to. You eat the food whether you like it or not. If you want to leave the nursing home, you need somebody to take you. If you're in a wheelchair like me, you need a wheelchair van at your disposal. Most commercial wheelchair vans need forty-eight hours notice if you want to go someplace, and they need an hour leeway for when they'll pick you up and bring you home. For a lot of people, a nursing home is where they need to be. But my mind is still good, and I am still accomplishing a lot of worthwhile things.

A nursing home may not be prison, but in my eyes, it's too close for comfort. So if you're trying to learn the technique of never giving up, you need to realize that there are consequences if you do give up. If you look hard at these consequences, you may become like me and never give up until you've exhausted every possibility.

There are many stories that I could tell you of accomplishments that required a miracle and a never-give-up attitude, but my best and most rewarding story is the series of events that have kept me out of a nursing home for almost twenty-four years. A large cast of people has helped me in this next-to-impossible task. The first time I was scheduled to go to the nursing home was when I was going to be released from the hospital after my accident. I already had my name on the nursing home's waiting list and had been staying in the hospital until there was an opening. I did not have much to do with this first brush with the nursing home. Lynda had decided that my family couldn't take care of me at home. But for some reason, at the last minute she changed her mind.

In the beginning, the cost for my attendants wasn't too bad, but as we hired more and more attendants, the cost increased steadily over the years. Lynda and I were able to make enough money to make the payroll and pay the rest of our living expenses until 1989. That was the year that I lost my insurance licenses. From that time on, our income went down, and there was a crisis to make the payroll almost every month. I wish I had kept a log of how I made the payroll each month. The stories are too numerous to tell. In fact, I don't even remember them all. Although I have never given up in my desire to stay out of a nursing home, I must add again that I have had a lot of help from family and friends. I think in some cases my attitude of not giving up might have influenced their choice to help me. For whatever reason, they helped me, and I thank them and I thank God.

Another time I was headed for a nursing home and had almost given up was right after my wife left. She stayed with me for seventeen years and was very instrumental in my quality of life and my chance to be with her and our children. I think it is amazing that she stayed with me for so many years. Lynda is a very private person, and living in our house was like living in a fish bowl. She needed to have time alone, and in our home that wasn't possible. Another reason she left was because of my gambling, and rightfully so. When Lynda left, I was very depressed and did not work as hard as I should have for the first month or so. Also, I had to hire a few more people, as she had always been there to help the other girls take care of me. I got way behind in my bills and was so broke I qualified for Medicaid for about three months. Medicaid paid for more than half of my attendants and I was on food stamps, but I was still going in the hole. At this time, I put my name on the waiting list for a nursing home again. I didn't want to go, but I thought I had better be prepared in case I could not pull out of my financial dilemma. A good friend of mine, Marv Skaar, organized a fundraising drive by sending out letters to my friends and, in some cases, acquaintances. Marv raised about twenty-five thousand dollars. I got off Medicaid and went back to work. Marv helped me escape again.

Things went pretty well for the next four years with minor miracles making the payroll month after month. Liz, a girl who worked for me for eleven years, told me I had better not let the other girls know what kind of financial shape I was in or they would panic, thinking they were not going to get their paycheck. Liz had seen many months where three or four days before the end of the month I still didn't know how I was going to make the payroll, but she never worried. She said she knew she would always get paid because I had never missed a payroll. At times, I had gotten behind in other bills, but I always knew that if I didn't pay my attendants, they'd be gone, and it would be all over. It's not that any of my attendants would've been unkind to me, but they needed their money to go to school and pay bills.

In 1998, I went down for the nine count again. This time my daughter, Mo, came to my rescue. To shorten a long story, I had a pressure sore that kept me in bed twenty-four hours a day, seven days a week. I had three surgeries on the pressure sore, and the first two were unsuccessful. My third surgery was finally successful. After that surgery, I was in the hospital for about five weeks. I left the hospital to lie at home in a special airbed that I had rented from a medical supply store. I normally sleep in a waterbed sitting up. I cannot begin to tell you how claustrophobic and helpless I feel when lying on my side in a bed. For month after month, I had to lie on my right side approximately twenty hours a day. Every four hours, I could lie on my back for an hour. The part of my right shoulder that I can feel would get so sore that it would go numb. The pain was excruciating.

During this time, I was still on the telephone trying to sell products, but it was very hard. Much of the time, my attendant was busy taking care of my wound, which took away from the time we normally spent on work. I was so far behind in my bills that I was constantly fending off creditors, especially the utilities people. My phones were shut off three or four times, and I would have to borrow money to get them hooked up again. I was continually behind in payments to the power company, but they never shut off the power. If they had, the airbed, which was run by electricity, would have gone flat, and my pressure sore would have been severely damaged. They worked with me to make sure the power was never shut off. I appreciate their sensitivity.

In September of 1998, I was almost healed and could be in my chair for a few hours each day. Each day, I was able to stay up longer and longer, and I was almost ready to go back to work. I was no longer disabled. I had gone from laying on my side or back twenty-four hours a day to only being paralyzed from the neck down and able to sit in my wheelchair again. My son, Mike, heard me say this and started using it in some motivating seminars he was giving. He told his audience that his quadriplegic father did not feel disabled once he was back in his wheelchair. Even the government was mesmerized by this phenomenon. I was way behind in my payroll taxes, and they knocked off all of the interest and penalties for the time that I was lying in bed "disabled." After I was able to get back in my wheelchair, they charged me interest and penalties, as I was now not "disabled."

I was close to one hundred thousand dollars in debt, and I did not see how I was ever going to pull out of it. Mo said she figured I deserved one more chance, so she organized a terrific fundraiser. It was a campaign of letters sent to about a thousand people and a fundraising banquet headlined by Ron Erhardt. Erhardt had been a coach at North Dakota State University in Fargo for many years. He left Fargo to be an assistant coach for the New England Patriots and eventually became the head coach for the Patriots. He was the offensive coordinator under head coach Bill Parcels when the New York Giants won two Super Bowls. Erhardt was then offensive coordinator for the Pittsburgh Steelers and is now retired. The emcee for the banquet was Boyd Christenson, a local radio and TV personality. My counselor, Reverend Brunsberg, gave the invocation. Entertainment was provided by the F-M Acroteam, a gymnastics organization that has performed for almost every NBA team and six or seven NBA all-star games, and was requested by Dr. Julius Erving to perform at half time of his final game in Philadelphia. My daughter, Mo, had been on one of the early teams, and I was one of the founding fathers. Lucy Thrasher, a noted opera singer in Fargo, also performed. They all put on a fantastic show.

The benefit received much publicity on local talk shows and on all of the regional TV sport shows. It was a roaring success. Besides all of my friends, who donated generously, I received many donations from people I did not know. Some of them have become friends. In fact, one of the investors in this book is Bruce Carr, who gave a five hundred dollar donation to send five people to the banquet who otherwise could not afford to go. The fundraiser and banquet ended up raising more than eighty thousand dollars. I was back in business again. As I said previously in this book and at the banquet, "All of my family, my caregivers, my friends, strangers, and certainly God, have helped me through these twenty-four years. I have a very strong belief in God and faith that everything happens for a reason. My accident happened because God had this mission for me." I think that my "never give up" attitude has been the catalyst to get me this far. I hope this book helps many thousands of people in the same way I have been helped. Maybe it will also help me finish my days in a more normal way. I have had enough of the roller-coaster rides and would like to wheel off into the sunset.

Shortly after I paid off most of my bills and was back at work full-time, I had another unexpected setback. I had an endoscopy in mid-1997. The doctor was looking for an ulcer and told me I had Barrett's disease of the esophagus. He put me on a prescription of two Prevacid a day and told me to come back in six months for another endoscopy. I had no idea how serious Barrett's disease could be. I didn't get back to the doctor in six months because of my yearlong battle with my pressure sore. So in December of 1998, I went in for another endoscopy. Several weeks later, the doctor called me back and told me I had Severe Dysplasia, or in layman's terms, pre-cancer of the esophagus. The doctor told me I would need to have my esophagus removed immediately because the pre-cancer was ready to transform to cancer. This is a very serious operation, and for a quadriplegic, it's much worse. They would have to remove my esophagus and stretch my stomach up eighteen inches to sew it to my throat. They also told me I would be on a respirator for quite some time, probably for life. Nursing home, here I come again. This story is starting to sound like a broken record, and it doesn't play sweet music. My surgery was scheduled for early January 1999. After the big high from the fundraiser, this was a low blow, and I was very depressed.

My daughter had a New Year's Eve party that year, and I really didn't want to go because I didn't feel like talking to anyone. But it was lonely at home, so I decided to go over for a little while. If this wasn't divine intervention, I've never seen it. At the party was a high school classmate of Mo's who is now an Eye, Ear, Nose and Throat Specialist named Dr. Sue Mathison. I told her about my upcoming surgery, and she said, "Tom, that's an awful surgery, especially for you (as a quadriplegic)." Sue told me about a patient she had seen recently who had the same problem and had gone to Abbott Northwestern Hospital in Minneapolis for laser treatments from Dr. Robert Ganz. This had happened more than a year ago, and he was still cancer free. I told Sue that I would like to see Dr. Ganz. She called the next day and made an appointment for me the day after that. It was now less than a week from the date of my surgery.

I went to visit Dr. Ganz. I met with him in his office with my attendant of eleven years Liz Fevig-Hager, my ex-wife Lynda, my daughter Kathleen, and an intern who happened to be from Fargo and knew my sons. Dr. Ganz explained the procedure. On Monday, I would be injected with a dye. On Wednesday, they would perform an endoscopy with a laser. The dye would light up the pre-cancerous areas, and Dr. Ganz would shoot the lighted areas with the laser. On Friday, he would do the same procedure for any pre-cancerous areas that might have been missed. Dr. Ganz said the laser treatment was still in the experimental stage, but there was an eighty to ninety percent chance that this procedure would be successful. For some reason, I said, "Can I think about it for a day?" I don't know why I said that, because I usually make fast decisions. Everybody in the room said, "Tom, what do you have to think about? This is a no-brainer." So I agreed and scheduled the procedure to start the following Monday. I went back to Fargo and canceled my surgery. After my first procedure, I had this treatment performed two more times to get small pre-cancerous areas that were still there. There was no hospitalization, and I could leave half an hour to an hour after the procedure. I only lost nine days from work and that was traveling to and from Minneapolis. In April 2001, I had a check-up with Dr. Ganz, and my esophagus looked fine. No Barrett's, and no pre-cancer. I don't have to go back for a year. One more time, I've persevered and continued to live in my own home. My fight against cancer was just another example of never giving up, combined with divine intervention.

It's amazing that I'm still alive and *not* kicking, but the Lord must have a reason to keep me around. I have had the last rites of the Catholic Church four times. The first time was in 1955 when I was hurt in a college football game. The first diagnosis was a concussion, and I was initially put in the health center at the college. I started feeling worse and called my best friend Jack Bernardy. He drove me to my hometown of Detroit Lakes, where I could see my long-time family physician, Dr. Rutledge. Dr. Rutledge immediately admitted me to St. Mary's Hospital. Shortly after being admitted to the hospital, my temperature reached 104 degrees. That's when I was given last rites number one. Dr. Rutledge diagnosed my condition as polio. Later, I was transferred to St. John's Hospital in Fargo, where Dr. Gustafson, a neurosurgeon, diagnosed my condition as infectious mononucleosis of the nervous system. I had double vision and my left leg and right arm were paralyzed for about three months. My double vision cleared up, and my left leg and right arm came back to ninety percent of what they had been. Last rites number two was given to me when I arrived at the hospital the morning of my car accident, July 21, 1977. During my first three months at St. Luke's Hospital, I had two code blues and almost died during each of them. I was given last rites three and four with each of the code blues.

Staying out of a nursing home for 24 years is my biggest example of never giving up. Here is an example of one of my smaller triumphs over the near impossible. When I was still in intensive care, my son had a high school football game. He was playing for the Shanley Deacons in Fargo. At that time, they were the most successful football school in North Dakota, and probably in the upper Midwest. My son, Mike, was a sophomore and wasn't starting, but it was parents' night, and I still wanted to go. I asked Dr. Robert Johnson, my neurosurgeon, if I could go to the game. He told me I was crazy and said no. I was on a respirator at the time, had a trachea, still had the halo on my head, and was on the Stryker frame. Using my will to never give up, I pleaded with Dr. Johnson, "Isn't there some way that I can go?" To shut me up, and knowing it wouldn't be possible, he said I could go under the following conditions: I go in an ambulance that was equipped for a respirator, and I had to have a doctor and RN present. Dr. Johnson knew that insurance would not cover the ambulance and that going to and from the game would probably cost $1,000. What he didn't know was that I knew the owner of the ambulance service. I talked him into giving me a free ambulance to use for the game. My wife was an RN, so all we needed was a doctor. Dr. Goltz was a close family friend and was the Eye, Ear, Nose and Throat doctor who had put in my trachea and came in several times a week to check on it. All of his children had gone to Shanley, so he readily agreed to go with us.

Word spread quickly that I would be at the game, and when the ambulance drove by the Shanley stands, I got a rousing cheer from the crowd that made me feel great. We parked in the end zone, and I had to remain in a semi-laying down position. At halftime, when they were introducing the parents out on the football field, they also introduced Lynda and me in the ambulance. It was a bad night for football because it was raining quite hard. I couldn't see the game very well through the windshield wipers. However, my son got into the game in the fourth quarter and scored a touchdown. Shanley won the game by a large margin. The next day, when Dr. Johnson found out that I had gone to the game, he was shocked that I had pulled it off.

The following story is not earth shattering, but it is another example of not giving up. About twenty-five years ago, two friends of mine, Ron and Sharon, were moving from Long Island, New York to Cleveland, Ohio. Ron had told me the date that they would arrive in Cleveland and have their phone hooked up. I had something important to talk to Ron about. I called information and asked for a new listing in Cleveland for Ron and Sharon Taddei. The operator said there was no such listing. I then asked to talk to her supervisor. The supervisor also said she could not find a new listing for Ron and Sharon. I told her I knew the phone was in and that I really had to talk to Ron, and asked her to look just a little bit more. She looked some more and found a work order that showed the phone was being put in that day. She told me she did not know if it was hooked up yet, but gave me the number. I called the number, and a man answered. I asked him if Ron was there. He put Ron on the phone. Ron said, "How did you get this number? The phone's only been hooked up for about five minutes, and the man from the phone company hasn't even made a test call yet." I told him how I got the number, and he said, "Day, you are the only person in the world who could have gotten this telephone number."

Several of my near impossible feats occurred at the Los Angeles Forum. The first one was the Democratic National Convention held in 1960. My friends, Norm, Jerry, and I drove to the Forum to see if we could get in. When we got there, there were thousands of people trying to get in and having no luck. Many secret service agents and police provided tight security around the building and at the doors. In those days, the Democratic presidential nominee had not already been picked. Four or five candidates were still vying for the Democratic nomination, but Lyndon B. Johnson and John F.

Kennedy were the main combatants. Each time a candidate would be nominated, supporters would march in a circle around the floor holding signs promoting their candidates. The major candidates all had plenty of their supporters at the convention. At that time, there was a phenomenon that doesn't exist today. Several states would nominate a favorite "son," even though this person had no chance to get the nomination.

One of these favorite sons was the governor of Rhode Island. There weren't enough supporters for him, so one of his assistants came outside to ask for volunteers to carry signs. We were to march in to demonstrate support for the governor and march back outside. Guess which three of us did not march out. We ditched our signs and slipped into the crowd. It proved to be an extremely interesting experience. John F. Kennedy barely edged out Lyndon B. Johnson for the Democratic nomination for president. There were some great speeches. Apparently, we were the only three who got in uninvited.

Another example of "don't give up, don't ever give up" or "try the impossible" is the following story. Norm, Jerry, and I had all played sports and were rabid sports fans. We had been to two or three Rose Bowls without having tickets. The papers would say the game was sold out, but we would always find scalpers and sometimes, if we waited until a few minutes before the game, tickets were sold for less than face value. We went to the NCAA Finals at the Cow Palace in San Francisco without tickets. The media said the game was already sold out. When we got to the game, it was not like the Rose Bowl, where there were plenty of scalpers. It was quite hard to find tickets. But we persisted, and after an hour, we finally got three tickets. In the finals, Ohio State beat California for the NCAA championship, and Cincinnati beat NYU for third place. The games were fun to see because many of the players involved became stars in the pros. John Havlicek, Jerry Lucas, and Jerry Siegfried were playing for Ohio State. Darrall Imhoff played center for California. Satch Sanders played for NYU, and Oscar Robertson was playing for Cincinnati. This has become such a big tournament that it is fun to look back and say that we were at an NCAA final.

Two years later, Norm, Jerry, and I were again headed for

another sporting event without tickets. This one turned out to be the granddaddy of the impossible. The Lakers played the Celtics in the sixth game of the NBA Finals at the Los Angeles Forum. The Lakers had beaten the Celtics at Boston to lead the series three to two. With the Lakers having a chance to win the championship at home, the game was a sell-out. We knew we could still get tickets even though it had been sold out because we had always gotten tickets in the past. We drove to the game and arrived about three hours early. Approximately five thousand people were milling around in front of the Los Angeles Forum. After an exhaustive search through the crowd, we found out that no one was selling tickets. Everyone wanted to buy tickets.

We had been to the Forum and knew the building quite well. We decided to try to sneak in through a side door that led to the Boston Celtics' dressing room. From there, we went up the stairs and came out on the main floor. We were just about to disappear into the crowd when two security guards caught us and escorted us out of the building. We found our way back to the group of people we had been visiting with. They congratulated us on a nice effort, but everyone agreed that we weren't going to see the game. Everyone, that is, except me. I had been looking across the freeway at a strip mall where there were five or six businesses that were all ticket brokers. They sold tickets to sporting events, plays, operas, etc. It was about six o'clock, and the twelve lanes of freeway (six lanes in either direction) were packed. I said that I was going to go over there just in case one of the businesses had some tickets. Everyone laughed and told me I was nuts. Norm also said I was nuts, but he decided to go with me so that I would not die alone on the freeway.

We had to climb a rather high fence to get to the shoulder of the freeway, run across six lanes of rush-hour traffic, climb the fence in the middle, run across six more lanes of traffic, and then climb the last fence. I still can't imagine how we made it. If you are wondering why we didn't drive over there, you have never been to Southern California. Even though this was 1962, it would have taken an hour to find a route over to the mall. We walked to the strip mall, and tried the first business. It was closed. The second one was closed; the third one was closed; but the fourth or fifth one had a light on in the back. It was closed, but I pounded on the door. A man came to the door, and I told him that he would probably think we were crazy, but we wondered if he had any tickets for the Lakers/Celtics game. He said, "You must be the luckiest guys in the world. I just got a call from a fellow who was coming by to get four tickets, and he told me he couldn't make it." He sold them to us for the regular price plus their normal commission, which was much less than we would've had to pay a scalper. Excited, Norm and I jumped and ran across the freeway back to our friend Jerry and the group we were visiting with. Needless to say, they were shocked. I sold the one remaining ticket for enough money to pay for all four of the tickets. We went to the game and had a great time, even though the Lakers lost. After that, we never assumed that there would always be tickets for big events. The only advantage I had over everyone else in the Forum's parking lot was that I was not afraid to fail. They all assumed that there would not be any tickets across the freeway, and most of the time, they would have been right. But as I said earlier, my strength is that I never give up until I have failed beyond a shadow of a doubt.

To give up and miss exciting experiences is the hard way. Many people fall into that rut. We try to avoid doing things and think that we are taking the easy way out, but we are really setting ourselves up for the hard way out. Sometimes these examples are very obvious, but other times they are very subtle. Going to those basketball games, Mike's football game, and getting into the Democratic National Convention allowed me to have experiences that have enriched my life. If I had not experienced them (which would seem to be the easy way out), I would have taken the hard way out. Some of my memories would be missing, the memories that became part of my political and sports history.

This principle of never giving up should be applied to all aspects of your life—your hidden handicaps, your dreams, and your desires. I guarantee it will make your life better because even if you don't succeed, you will feel good about giving it your best shot. And the truth is you will succeed more often than you think is possible.

Chapter 13

WHO PUT THE TREE IN THE
MIDDLE OF THE ROAD

Now that you've read the book, where do you go from here? Let's take a quick look at the path I took. If you recall, after I graduated from high school, I started my college days of cheating and stealing tests. Other kids drank to rebel from home-life, but I chose a different path in rebellion against my father. My dad had came from a dysfunctional father, and he passed on dysfunctional habits to me. I carried this baggage into my adult life. I never got caught stealing the tests, and in my subconscious, I felt I was invincible. I never thought of the consequences of my actions. Because I never got caught doing anything that was wrong and irresponsible, the consequences just kept getting pushed farther ahead. Where did that lead me?

It took me ten years to finish a four-year degree. I later fell into a gambling addiction, where I squandered away everything I had earned. I ruined what could have been a great marriage and led my wife and kids through a dysfunctional nightmare they did not deserve and are still recovering from. Thank God they have all done a good job of recovering.

In my business life, I lived on the edge and made many bad decisions that cost me millions. I kept playing Russian roulette by driving when I was tired until finally I fired the gun and the bullet was in the chamber, leaving me paralyzed from the neck down. My car accident was a consequence of me believing I was indestructible, but I didn't recognize it as a consequence at the time. I thought it was an "accident."

Throughout it all, I continued to gamble. Even though I was

getting healthier mentally in some ways, the gambling prevented my full recovery. In 1990, when I lost my life insurance licenses in Minnesota and North Dakota, I finally hit bottom. I admitted defeat and took action by going to counseling every week. But again, gambling was still holding me back. I had to go through the next three of the four steps of eliminating a hidden handicap, which took seven more years.

Let's go over the steps of eliminating hidden handicaps. The first step, and probably the hardest in some cases, is to identify the hidden handicap. Many people have problems and don't realize what's causing them. For example, people don't always realize that they have a drinking problem or that they are depressed. Other problems, such as claustrophobia, are easy to identify. After you identify the problem, the next step is to admit that it's a serious problem that is affecting your life and the people around you. Some of these problems are very hard to admit, such as drinking and gambling. One of the reasons for this is that there are people who drink and gamble who don't have problems. After you have identified the hidden handicap and admitted that it's a serious problem to yourself, step three is to take action to correct it, which means you have to admit it to another person. The more people you tell, the bigger your chances to take action. The fourth and final step is going to a counselor or other type of professional to get help in understanding and eliminating the hidden handicap. Remember that in order for them to be able to help you, it is absolutely crucial for you to be one hundred percent honest with them. Eliminating hidden handicaps can be a very tough job. As I've said before, many hidden handicaps are harder to overcome than physical disabilities.

For being a guy everyone says is extremely smart, I sure didn't catch on to my hidden handicaps very quickly. This is worth repeating. If your family and friends say you have a problem, believe them and seek help. You'll save yourself all the emotional pain I have put many people through, including myself. I was too smart for my own good. I was able to rationalize and out argue anyone who told me I had a problem. Hopefully, you are smarter than I was.

I wish I could have read this book when I was in my twenties or thirties. Besides reading it, I also would have had to believe it and understand it so that I could have gone to counseling and changed my ways then, instead of thirty-some years later. Had I understood it and changed my ways, I would have felt as good then as I do now, or even better because I am still trying to rid myself of all the guilt. I have gotten rid of a lot of it, but ridding myself of it all is difficult. One of the answers is don't do things that make you feel guilty.

Another answer is don't ignore warning signs when they're put up in the middle of the road. A friend of mine who ran into an oak tree after having too many drinks said, "I'd like to get my hands on the guy who put that tree in the middle of the road." What actually happened was his car hit a tree in the ditch and was totaled. This individual thinks he was lucky that he didn't get a DUI. How he got out of the DUI is another story in itself that won't be told here. The sad part of this story is that my friend thinks he is lucky because he didn't get a DUI. The fact of the matter is he was extremely unlucky. Had he gotten a DUI, he would have been forced to go to alcohol counseling and maybe would have stopped driving while drinking. Instead, because he got away with this accident, he probably kept drinking and driving. This is a good example of someone ignoring the real cause of the problem at hand. And this is what you're doing when you avoid the signs. What you want to avoid is telling a story similar to mine thirty years from now. You may write it, or you may tell it, but you'll be wishing like Christmas past that you could go back in time and change your life. We all would like to go back and change things. But you can't change what happened one minute ago.

So what's the answer? There are many answers. Listen to people who have made mistakes and can help you avoid them. Another answer is to go to counseling now. If you're in your teens, twenties, thirties, forties, fifties, sixties, or seventies, go now. It's never too early, and it's never too late. Tell the counselor everything that you've ever done in your life as if your life depended on it because there's a good chance that a happy life does depend on it. Going to counseling is not dumb. It's not a weakness. And it doesn't mean that you can't take care of yourself. On the contrary, it is a very smart decision. After all, we have our teeth checked every six months, we have our cars checked annually, and many people go in for an annual physical. However, this physical is usually a checkup from the neck down. Don't you think you should have a checkup from the neck up?

My hope in writing this book is that when you see yourself in it, you will recognize that you have a hidden handicap and begin to work on eliminating it immediately. If you don't see yourself in this book, you are an extraordinary human being. However, if you do see yourself, begin by telling a friend and going to counseling. When you go to the counselor, remember, TELL THE WHOLE TRUTH. I didn't tell the truth initially about my gambling problem, and it held my complete recovery back for those seven years. If the counselor says you don't have a hidden handicap, you haven't lost anything. On the other hand, if you have a problem and don't go to counseling, it's a huge mistake. If you're going to make a mistake, make one that doesn't hurt you or anyone around you.

Since many of you have physical disabilities and most of you have hidden handicaps, I think many of you were able to see yourself someplace in this book. The book will be a success if only a few of you are helped. But I am an optimistic person. I hope that you are all helped. In order to be helped, you must have an open mind and want to feel better. It's hard to believe that many people don't want to feel better. Many would rather be miserable and then complain and drag others down with them.

Overcoming hidden handicaps is hard work, but once you succeed, you'll feel so much better about yourself. You'll also notice that other people feel much better about you. I have found that if you have hidden handicaps and don't tell anyone about them, they get bigger and bigger. As you start telling people about them, they get smaller and smaller, much like problems between people. If you have a disagreement with another person and don't talk about it, it becomes bigger and bigger. Other issues enter in until the people involved don't even remember the original problem. If you talk about it right away, you usually find that there were some misunderstandings and that it's not a big problem at all. Learn to communicate.

Communication makes everything better. The more you communicate with other people the better you're going to feel.

I have stated in this book on a couple of occasions that hidden handicaps are harder to overcome than physical disabilities. I have also said that hidden handicaps can be more painful *psychologically* than physical disabilities. First of all, I know that this is not true in every case. The important point is that when I said I got over my physical handicap quicker than I got over my hidden handicap, I meant the following. With my physical handicap, I was able to adjust to being in a wheelchair, and I was able to learn how to work and be a worthwhile member of society again. I also said I was working to overcome my hidden handicaps. If I get over all my hidden handicaps, I will still be a quad. I didn't mean to insinuate that this is an easy thing to be. I meant that I have adjusted to living life with a severe disability. For those of you with hidden handicaps and no physical disabilities, you should have more motivation to get rid of your pain than a person adjusting to their severe physical disabilities because if you have a painful hidden handicap, you may be in more psychological pain than I am, but if you are able to overcome that hidden handicap, you are now a happy, able-bodied person. So the moral of the story for all of us is don't ever give, take the easy way out, and overcome your hidden handicaps.

I got a lot out of writing this book. I hope that you got a lot out of reading it. May the rest of your life be as good as you can make it, and remember the rest of your life starts right now . . . now . . . now . . . now . . .

To order additional copies of
I TOOK THE EASY WAY OUT
please complete the following.

$19.95 EACH
*(plus $3.95 shipping & handling for first book,
add $2.00 for each additional book ordered.*

*Shipping and Handling costs for larger quantites
available upon request.*

Please send me _____ additional books at $19.95 + shipping & handling

Bill my: ❑ VISA ❑ MasterCard   Expires _____

Card # _____

Signature _____

Daytime Phone Number _____

For credit card orders call 1-888-568-6329
TO ORDER ON-LINE VISIT: www.jmcompanies.com
OR SEND THIS ORDER FORM TO:
McCleery & Sons Publishing
PO Box 248
Gwinner, ND 58040-0248

I am enclosing $_____   ❑ Check ❑ Money Order
Payable in US funds. No cash accepted.

SHIP TO:
Name_____

Mailing Address _____

City _____

State/Zip _____

Orders by check allow longer delivery time.
Money order and credit card orders will be shipped within 48 hours.
This offer is subject to change without notice.

New Releases

The Garlic Cure

Learn about natural breakthroughs to outwit: Allergies, Arthritis, Cancer, Candida Albicans, Colds, Flu and Sore Throat, Environmental and Body Toxins, Fatigue, High Cholesterol, High Blood Pressure and Homocysteine and Sinus Headaches. The most comprehensive, factual and brightly written health book on garlic of all times. INCLUDES: 139 GOURMET GARLIC RECIPES!
Written by James F. Scheer, Lynn Allison and Charlie Fox (240 pgs.)
$14.95 each in a 6x9" paperback.

For Your Love

Janelle, a spoiled socialite, has beauty and breeding to attract any mate she desires. She falls for Jared, an accomplished man who has had many lovers, but no real love. Their hesitant romance follows Jared and Janelle across the ocean to exciting and wild locations. Join in a romance and adventure set in the mid-1800's in America's grand and proud Southland.
Written by Gunta Stegura (358 pgs.)
$16.95 each in a 6x9" paperback.

Blessed Are The Peacemakers

A rousing tale that traces the heroic Rit Gatlin from his enlistment in the Confederate Army in Little Rock to his tragic loss of leg in a Kentucky battle, to his return in the Ozarks. He becomes engaged in guerilla warfare with raiders who follow no flag but their own. Rit finds himself involved with a Cherokee warrior, slaves and romance in a land ravaged by war.
By Joe W. Smith (444 pgs.)
$19.95 each in a 6 x 9 paperback

New Releases

Home Front
Read the continuing story of Carrie Amundson, whose life in North Dakota began in *Bonanza Belle*. This is the story of her family, faced with the challenges, sacrifices and hardships of World War II. Everything changed after the Pearl Harbor attack, and ordinary folk all across America, on the home front, pitched in to help in the war effort. Even years after the war's end, the effects of it are still evident in many of the men and women who were called to serve their country. Written by Elaine Ulness Swenson. (304 pgs.) $15.95 each in a 6x8-1/4" paperback.

Seasons With Our Lord
Original seasonal and special event poems written from the heart. Feel the mood with the tranquil color photos facing each poem. A great coffee table book or gift idea. Written by Cheryl Lebahn Hegvik. (68 pgs.) $24.95 each in a 11x8-1/2 paperback.

Whispers in the Darkness
In this fast paced, well thought out mystery with a twist of romance, Betty Pearson comes to a slow paced, small town. Little did she know she was following a missing link - what the dilapidated former Beardsley Manor she was drawn to, held for her. With twists and turns, the Manor's secrets are unraveled. Written by Shirlee Taylor. (88 pgs.) $14.95 each in a 6x9" paperback.

Outward Anxieity - Inner Calm
Steve Crociata is known to many as the Optician to the Stars. He was diagnosed with a baffling form of cancer. The author has processed experiences in ways which uniquely benefit today's readers. We learn valuable lessons on how to cope with distress, how to marvel at God, and how to win at the game of life. By Steve Crociata (334 pgs.) $19.95 each in a 6 x 9 paperback

Pycnogenol®
Pycnogenol® for Superior Health presents exciting new evidence about nature's most powerful antioxidant. Pycnogenol® improves your total health, reduces risk of many diseases, safeguards your arteries, veins and entire circulation system. It protects your skin - giving it a healthier, smoother younger glow. Pycnogenol® also boosts your immune system. Read about it's many other beneficial effects. Written by Richard A. Passwater, Ph.D. (122 pgs.) $5.95 each in a 4-1/8 x 6-7/8" paperback.

Home In One Piece

While working alone on his parent's farm one January morning in 1992, eighteen year old John Thompson became entangled in a piece of machinery. Both arms were ripped from his body and he was knocked unconscious. He was awakened by his dog, got off the ground, and staggered to the house. John opened a door with his mouth and grasped a pen in his teeth to call for help on the phone. A truthful journey with themes of survival, recovery and enduring hope. By John Thompson as told to Paula Crain Grosinger, RN. (162 pgs.) $16.95 each in a 6 x 9 paperback.

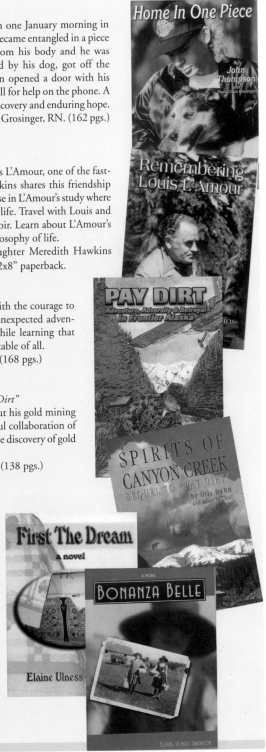

Remembering Louis L'Amour

Reese Hawkins was a close friend of Louis L'Amour, one of the fastest selling writers of all time. Now Hawkins shares this friendship with L'Amour's legion of fans. Sit with Reese in L'Amour's study where characters were born and stories came to life. Travel with Louis and Reese in the 16 photo pages in this memoir. Learn about L'Amour's lifelong quest for knowledge and his philosophy of life. Written by Reese Hawkins and his daughter Meredith Hawkins Wallin. (178 pgs.) $16.95 each in a 5-1/2x8" paperback.

Pay Dirt

An absorbing story reveals how a man with the courage to follow his dream found both gold and unexpected adventure and adversity in Interior Alaska, while learning that human nature can be the most unpredictable of all. Written by Otis Hahn & Alice Vollmar. (168 pgs.) $15.95 each in a 6x9" paperback.

Spirits of Canyon Creek *Sequel to "Pay Dirt"*

Hahn has a rich stash of true stories about his gold mining experiences. This is a continued successful collaboration of battles on floodwaters, facing bears and the discovery of gold in the Yukon. Written by Otis Hahn & Alice Vollmar. (138 pgs.) $15.95 each in a 6x9" paperback.

First The Dream

This story spans ninety years of Anna's life. She finds love, loses it, and finds it once again. A secret that Anna has kept is fully revealed at the end of her life. Written by Elaine Ulness Swenson. (326 pgs.) $15.95 each in a 6x8-1/4" paperback

Bonanza Belle

In 1908, Carrie Amundson left her home to become employed on a bonanza farm. One tragedy after the other befell her and altered her life considerably and she found herself back on the farm. Written by Elaine Ulness Swenson. (344 pgs.) $15.95 each in a 6x8-1/4" paperback.

Dr. Val Farmer's Honey, I Shrunk The Farm

The first volume in a three part series of Rural Stress Survival Guides discusses the following in seven chapters: Farm Economics; Understanding The Farm Crisis; How To Cope With Hard Times; Families Going Through It Together; Dealing With Debt; Going For Help, Helping Others and Transitions Out of Farming.
Written by Val Farmer. (208 pgs.)
$16.95 each in a 6x9" paperback.

Country-fied

Stories with a sense of humor and love for country and small town people who, like the author, grew up country-fied . . . Country-fied people grow up with a unique awareness of their dependence on the land. They live their lives with dignity, hard work, determination and the ability to laugh at themselves.
Written by Elaine Babcock. (184 pgs.)
$14.95 each in a 6x9" paperback.

Charlie's Gold and Other Frontier Tales

Kamron's first collection of short stories gives you adventure tales about men and women of the west, made up of cowboys, Indians, and settlers.
Written by Kent Kamron. (174 pgs.)
$15.95 each in a 6x9" paperback.

A Time For Justice

This second collection of Kamron's short stories takes off where the first volume left off, satisfying the reader's hunger for more tales of the wide prairie.
Written by Kent Kamron. (182 pgs.)
$16.95 each in a 6x9" paperback.

It Really Happened Here!

Relive the days of farm-to-farm salesmen and hucksters, of ghost ships and locust plagues when you read Ethelyn Pearson's collection of strange but true tales. It captures the spirit of our ancestors in short, easy to read, colorful accounts that will have you yearning for more.
Written by Ethelyn Pearson. (168 pgs.)
$24.95 each in an 8-1/2x11" paperback.

(Add $3.95 shipping & handling for first book, add $2.00 for each additional book ordered.)

Prayers For Parker Cookbook - *Parker Sebens is a 3 year old boy from Milnor, ND, who lost both of his arms in a tragic farm accident on September 18, 2000. He has undergone many surgeries to reattach his arms, but because his arms were damaged so extensively and the infection so fierce, they were unable to save his hands. Parker will face many more surgeries in his future, plus be fitted for protheses.*
This 112 pg. cookbook is a project of the Country Friends Homemakers Club from Parker's community. All profits from the sale of this book will go to the Parker Sebens' Benefit Fund, a fund set up to help with medical-related expenses due to Parker's accident. $8.00 ea. in a 5-1/4"x8-1'4" spiral bound book.